Facing Cancer

A Spiritual Journey from Pain to Peace

Meredith McNerney

INFINITY
PUBLISHING

Copyright © 2009 by Meredith McNerney

ISBN 978-0-7414-5547-5

All scripture quotations, unless otherwise indicated, are taken from the Contemporary English Version.

Published by:

INFINITY
PUBLISHING

INFINITY PUBLISHING
1094 New DeHaven Street, Suite 100
West Conshohocken, PA 19428-2713
Info@buybooksontheweb.com
www.buybooksontheweb.com
Toll-free (877) BUY BOOK
Local Phone (610) 941-9999
Fax (610) 941-9959

Printed in the United States of America
Published March 2014

Acknowledgments

To God...
Thank you for teaching me how to savor life.

To My Parents...
Your belief in me never wavered. Your love for me created security and self-esteem deep within my soul.

To My Husband...
My happiest moments have been spent laughing with you. You make me a better person.

To My Daughters...
You are the two most important reasons to fight. I am the luckiest mother in the world.

To My Brothers...
I will always be your "little sister" and for that I am proud. Thank you for always encouraging me.

To Ellyn...
Without you this book would not be complete. Your dedication and expertise will help me to spread an important message – a message of hope. Thank you for the countless hours you devoted to seeing me from start to finish! Thank you for an awesome, God-inspired friendship.

To Mom and Dad McNerney...
Your faith is unshakable. What a blessing it is to be a part of your family.

To Steve and Ronya...
Many times your lives were interrupted to take care of Mark, the girls, and me. Thank you for your friendship, love, and never-ending support.

To My Dear Friends Who Run *A Message of Hope Cancer Fund (MHCF)*...
Tracey, Linda, Elizabeth, Melissa, Missy, Sally, Brandi, and Darlene I am so honored that you believed in me from the start. I am so impressed by what each of you has accomplished for our fund. With you, I am strong. Because of your support, many families who thought they had lost it all now have hope. You each add to my life in a special way and I could never imagine going through life without you.

To The Many Volunteers and Supporters of MHCF...
Thank you for helping our vision to become a reality. Without our volunteers, our success would be limited.

To My Beautiful Girlfriends...
I have grown with each of you in countless ways. I am blessed to be friends for a lifetime.

To Steve Simon...
Thank you for your belief in this project. I truly appreciate all of the time you've dedicated to helping me share this message.

To The Amazing Staff at Highland Elementary School...
I am inspired by you! What a wonderful experience it has been to return to the field of education.

To My Entire Family...
How could one girl be so lucky to have so many amazing people in her life? I love each of you deeply.

To anyone facing cancer – never lose hope.

INTRODUCTION

Jesus turned. He saw the woman and said,
"Don't worry! You are now well because of your faith."
At that moment she was healed.

Matthew 9:22

"I will call you the moment I know something," the familiar voice reassures me. "It will be about a week." Tears filled my eyes and my throat tightened. I left the office once again...and waited. The idea of *learning* to wait has become all too familiar.

When you live with cancer you must learn to live without instant decisions or news. Sometimes we wait for test results, to see if radiation worked, for our hair to return after chemotherapy, or to simply feel human again. At the moment, I'm in a constant state of waiting – will my cancer return?

It's like mastering a new skill, such as driving or swimming. But we only acquire this skill when we *choose* to. And in all this waiting I've made an important realization: life really is all about learning how to wait. I ask my young daughters to wait when they want to use the computer and I am answering emails. We wait in line at the store and wait for the work day to be over.

I had to wait to meet the man of my dreams while dating some others who essentially helped me define what I really wanted in a man. It took a year of trying and waiting to become pregnant for the first time. I remember how hard it was to wait each month and then read a negative result when we so desperately wanted a baby. Then, my husband and I

1

couldn't wait until the day both of our daughters slept through the night without interrupting our sleep. Now we can't wait until they are both in school and we no longer have a daycare bill - I've been waiting for extra money to decorate our bedroom.

Then there's the waiting of more serious issues like waiting to see if the latest interventions are working for a young boy with autism whose parents want nothing more than to help him live a full life. Or watching a loved one slowly die from the complications associated with old age and waiting for the day they can rest in peace. Or a divorced man trying to rebuild his life and waiting to see if he'll ever reconnect with his children. For me, I'm waiting to find out if I have cancer again. Waiting to find out what lies ahead.

Cancer can be anything that takes you out of the present. It is not just a medically-diagnosed disease. We've all dealt with our own painful circumstances - our own "cancer" - and while we wait for those circumstances to get better, we are missing out on the present. "Cancer" can be many things. It can be your inability to forgive someone who wronged you. It can be the worry that fills your soul over an issue in which you have no control. It can be your negative attitude about money, or health, or even a strained relationship with a family member. Cancer is everywhere because many people choose to live with it. Many of us spend our lives living with "cancer" - one that robs us of our joy, hope, and love - and then we miss out on the present.

Personally, I decided to replace peace with my pain. In the end I realize it's not the *waiting* we should focus on at all. In our quest for answers, we often lose sight of what life is really all about - the present. I strive to enjoy each moment of my life as if it were my last. In essence, I choose to live in the present because I don't want to miss out on the beautiful life that surrounds me. When we live outside of the present, we live with our own cancer.

Yes, I am a cancer survivor. Not because I fought off Merkel Cell Cancer once, but because I made peace with the enemy. Merkel Cell will not destroy me, who I am, what I do, or how I live. Merkel Cell has made me stronger – more grateful. My hope is that you too will face your own cancer; whether it is a medically-diagnosed cancer or a cancer that lives in your mind. Because when you embrace all of the waiting and find peace in the present, then you are truly living.

1

SPIRITUAL LAYERS

If you obey and do right, a light will show you the way and fill you with happiness.

Psalm 97:11

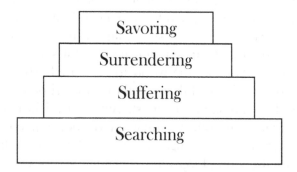

| Savoring |
| Surrendering |
| Suffering |
| Searching |

I haven't always been comfortable sharing my faith – my spirituality and relationship with God – with strangers! Over time and after many painful experiences, I began to realize that if I became completely transparent and honest my story may actually help someone find hope during their own dark times. Besides, I must admit that the story itself is pretty unique and a bit inspiring; and as a result, it may restore peace in a few broken-hearted people. So, after putting all of my fear aside and burying the worry that comes from being completely honest about my personal failures and victories, I decided that the risk would be worth it if I positively impacted even just one person. Above all, I pray that you will take away something meaningful after sharing in my personal journey from pain to peace.

To begin with, most of my friends would probably tell you that I am deeply connected to God, always talking about prayer, and fairly religious. At the same time, they will tell you that I love to have fun and laugh a lot, occasionally drink too much and tell crazy stories, and that (like many women) I love to shop. And they are right on all accounts!

From my perspective, my life is very full; I love God very much; and my relationship with God is not complicated at all. It is true that I have endured my fair share of pain and not just the pain that comes with facing cancer, but pain from other horrible illnesses and many of life's challenges. With that being said, I am never afraid to have a good time. I do have a fairly extensive collection of shoes, and in many ways I am a very ordinary girl! Coupled with my playful side comes the fact that my kids mean the world to me...my husband is my best friend...and I couldn't live without my girlfriends. So on many levels, I am similar to most. But what might make me different than some others is that my relationship with God, which has grown and changed a lot over the years, is literally one of love, freedom, forgiveness, laughter, and peace.

Have you ever tried a new product and fallen in love? You know what I mean...a product that actually works, makes your life easier, and has definitely made you happier after using it. What if that product also created a healthy habit within you, had a lasting positive effect on you, actually helped you reach your full-potential in life, and best of all, was available free of charge to you and everyone around you...Would you tell your friends and family that they should begin using it? Would you convince them to trust you until they gave it a try for themselves? I would. And with this book, that is exactly what I hope to do. Share. Share the most precious discovery I've ever made in my life - my personal relationship with Jesus. And at the risk of sounding like someone I am not - you will not see me standing on your doorstep with a bible in my hand, nor am I ever going to preach on city streets to get my message across - I simply have a desire to share what is normally so private to me because my relationship with God is my "product" for life. Prayer, especially, is the part of my life that is most important to me. Let me begin by sharing how all of this started.

If you are like me, you probably love to eat and will hopefully be able to make sense of my spiritual analogy. Building faith is a lot like building a wedding cake. You can't build a solid cake without a strong foundation. Each layer is important. Each layer is different. Each layer is a part of the whole finished product. Growing in faith requires moving through each layer of spirituality.

My spiritual cake consists of four main layers, chocolate layers by the way! Your cake may require different layers, a more personalized flavor, but ultimately the best gift is found in the top layer! My cake is layered with a bit of searching, a lot of suffering, some much-needed surrendering, and bitter-sweet savoring. Savoring, of course, is the best part and is my favorite layer. It's in this layer that I can clearly see both the beauty and pain in my life. Through my joy and sorrow I am a stronger, more loving person.

As a fulfilled spiritual woman today, I am now able to live a full life with purpose, meaning, and happiness. Maybe you can't see that for yourself right now. Perhaps your life is full of complicated relationships, pain and suffering, or just too much negativity! I agree that life is difficult, but I hope that you'll consider building your own spiritual layers in order to live your life to its fullest.

I invite you to begin by asking yourself a few questions:

1. When was the last time you felt completely whole and satisfied with your life?

2. When was the last time you really laughed and relaxed?

3. How deeply connected do you feel to yourself and the people around you?

4. How well do you know God?

I have to be honest and admit that I'm not a trained theologian. And with all due respect to all of the experts out there, I just think that sometimes we learn best from the most ordinary, average people who have a story to share. I share my journey from pain to peace because I feel called to spread a message of hope. I've witnessed so much pain and suffering and have endured my own share without a doubt. But along the way, I've learned to enjoy a much sweeter life.

My life has not always been easy. By the time I was 31, I had faced a deadly cancer, overcome debilitating vertigo that came with two brain surgeries, lost my left kidney to kidney disease, and endured more common suffering like c-sections, break-ups, and a sagging butt! Yet, somehow, I found God in all of my pain.

I imagine you have a story, too. Do you think it's too difficult or insignificant to share? I'm here to encourage you – to let you know that your story is important because it belongs to you. I hope that by sharing my life with you, you will think about your own story and begin to build your own spiritual cake.

Throughout my journey, I've rediscovered who I am and the meaning of my life. I know for sure that my most difficult trials have been purposeful which ultimately means that the plan for my life is perfect – as is yours. I believe we're on this earth to enjoy life – to savor each part – but that our *lives* get in the way of our *living*. It wasn't until I was faced with death, that I learned how to fully live my life. Isn't that both wonderful and sad?

I know from my experience that many survivors (survivors of illness, divorce, abuse, or any other pain) feel that way. The most fulfilled people I know are often those who have suffered the most.

My belief in God and my evolved faith has developed a lot over the years. It seems that with each painful experience, I found myself working through my feelings in *layers*.

As I watch people around me, talk with co-workers or friends, and share experiences with family, I realize that we don't savor life the way God intended! We are generally unhappy, dissatisfied, worried, upset, or incomplete. And I have felt all of those feelings. But, spirituality is watching yourself evolve into who God created you to be and recognizing yourself along the way. In building my own spiritual cake, I realized that the best part of the journey has been discovering who I am in each layer.

In the first layer, the largest part of my spiritual cake, I found myself **searching**. For most people, the layer in which we are searching is the heaviest and hardest layer to break through. This is similar to a wedding cake. The first layer – the bottom layer – is the foundation on which the cake is built. Without the first layer there could be no second layer and so forth. Therefore, we can never fully experience God until we begin searching for Him.

While searching, we tend to ask ourselves many hard questions such as:

- Who is God, really?

- If God is all loving and kind, why do we suffer?

- Who am I?

- Is Jesus really an important or necessary part in building a relationship with God?

- What if there isn't a God?

- Why do bad things happen to good people?

- Why are some *Christians* rude, hurtful, impatient, or judgmental?

- What do the rules of religion have to do with me being a spiritual person?

- What is my purpose on this earth?

- Does God love me?

- Am I truly forgiven for my past?

- How do I seek or find forgiveness?

- What is peace anyway?

- How do I know if God really cares about me?

- What makes me happy?

Wow! What an overwhelming list. I've asked myself all of those questions at some point in my life. I know for sure that searching for God while trying to find myself was an important first step to my faith journey.

My faith journey and life experiences brought me from searching to **suffering** many times. As I share my story, it will become obvious that my life became so personally difficult that I finally gave up control and learned to **surrender**. Only after surrendering, experiencing more suffering and surrendering again, did I learn to **savor** life.

For me, I can finally look back and understand that my suffering played the most important role in my life. I often felt ripped apart during the most difficult parts of my journey – broken and shred to pieces. But I realize now that as a result of my suffering I was able to build a new life; a life worth savoring.

When designing a wedding cake, the baker reminds the couple to save the top layer and wait to savor it on their first anniversary. That top layer is meant to be the most special and is saved in an effort to enjoy it after the chaos of the wedding day is long gone.

Savoring life today is about being peaceful every day. I am a pretty average person. My husband and I are raising two daughters, we both work full-time as teachers, and we live life on a budget. My happiness is not a result of fame, money, success, or accomplishments. But I am finally satisfied and peaceful. I have always been a very energetic person with a "Type A" personality – a personality that forces me to overdo, or search for more. With that being said, I am still the same person today; but the difference is I am able to savor each part of my life by allowing God to guide its direction.

Often I would wait until a goal was met, and then recognize how great it was or feel good about myself only when I had accomplished things. I still love to create lists and it feels so good to cross things off when I am done; but on the other hand, I now find joy in the present. I don't *wait* to savor life.

My goals and dreams today are bigger than ever, but my focus is on savoring every part of the dream; not waiting until it comes true to start living, but loving life at every stage.

My journey has been worth it because through all of the pain I found God waiting for me, ready to teach me how to savor my life. Although I doubted God at times, and wondered why my life turned out to be so difficult, the lessons I gained were well worth the grievous experiences.

Whatever process you will go through, however long it takes, I pray that you experience the top layer of your cake. So that you look at yourself and think: *I am truly in love with God, in love with myself, and in love with the people around me.*

It took me a long time, a lot of pain, and many lessons – some I had to learn three or four times – to make it to the layer in which I am able to savor life. Your journey will be different, but it is just as important, and God's love for you is just as strong.

Don't ever give up while you are searching. Remember, you are loved. According to the Bible, a "mustard seed" of faith is all you need in order to receive God's love. That's it. Thank goodness because sometimes a mustard seed was all the faith I had! He certainly wants and desires a personal relationship with all of us, but He is so loving, so forgiving, and so kind that He loves you even if you are still searching for Him.

At times, I am still searching. I find myself slipping away – feeling lost and searching again. But the beauty of having a solid spiritual foundation is that you are never alone. It's much easier to reconnect with God when you already know Him.

Each day, I seek His guidance, assurance, peace, love, and forgiveness to ensure that my mind stays focused on God. As a result, most of the time, I am able to fully savor my life because He's helped me reach a new level of spirituality that came only as a result of working through many layers. It is in my top layer that I can savor life with my family, friends, and you. That's right - part of my top layer is savoring my experiences with *you*. I hope that my story - my journey from pain to peace - will inspire you in some small way.

2

LOVE

No one has ever seen God. But if we love each other,
God lives in us, and his love is truly in our hearts.

1 John 4:12

In order to fully share my journey, I must begin from the beginning.

I was born on February 26th, 1976 to two adoring parents. I have heard the story over and over again – my mom missed one pill and I was her surprise baby! "The best surprise we could have ever had," she would say as she finished the story. "When your father found out you were a girl he went crazy; pink blankets, pink hats, and pink balloons. It was all pink."

"When you were born they first brought you out in a blue blanket," she would tell me, "but your father insisted that you were sent back to the nurses to be rewrapped in pink. You were his little girl from the first moment he laid eyes on you."

My parents were married at age 18 and by all material standards had nothing – absolutely nothing. No college degree, minimal opportunity, and certainly not a lot of money. They were in love and to them that was all that mattered. My oldest brother, Mike, was born exactly nine months after they were married and within five years, my parents had my two brothers and me – Michael, Mark, and Meredith. I was the youngest and the only girl. I really had it made! I remember one of the only times my daddy ever yelled at me (which I deserved) he sent me a bouquet of flowers the next day to tell me he loved me. Every girl should be so lucky. Isn't it every little girl's dream to be so loved? I was. I believe I still am.

Yet, I was often sick as a baby. As I became plagued by projectile vomiting and diarrhea, both my mom and dad fought hard for answers. Despite tests and doctors' appointments, it wasn't clear, at first, what exactly was going on.

However by the time I was two months old, one pediatrician found a clue by studying my right ear. My little ear, as my parents called it, seemed only like a unique part of me – but certainly not the answer to the unexplained illness. To everyone's surprise, my "little ear" provided more information than expected. Since our ears and kidneys run on the same chromosome, it was likely that the deformed ear would offer information about possible kidney disease.

Keep in mind, the right side of the brain controls muscles on the left side of the body and vice versa. Therefore, damage to one side of the brain will affect the opposite side of the body. As a result, it was discovered that my left kidney wasn't functioning properly and that diagnosis became the reason why my childhood was surrounded by kidney infections.

And although I endured several, painful kidney infections each year, my life wasn't that much different from most of my peers. In an effort to keep my childhood as "normal" as possible, my parents kept me involved in a lot of activities – particularly dance lessons. My mom owned several dance studios in our hometown, so it seemed only natural that I would take a liking to ballet, tap, and jazz. I competed and enjoyed every aspect of competition. I learned to win gracefully and accept defeat respectfully. Often I felt well enough to participate, but occasionally the infections would cause an unexpected disruption.

When I was six years old, my parents entered me in a local beauty pageant. I wanted to be crowned "Little Miss Valentine" so I could wear the faux mink coat that was given as a part of the first prize package! I laugh today at the memory of that particular day because my brothers – who are much more competitive than I am – took the approach of adding negative slander towards the other contestants in an effort to help me believe I would win. They pumped me up and I was ready to fight for that crown. (Yes, I realize how ridiculous this all sounds!)

That day, I was crowned Little Miss Valentine. My brothers, my mother, and my father were so proud. I was excited because I got to take home a crown and that little faux mink shawl – which I still have. I was thrilled!

Quickly the excitement of the day turned to panic after returning home only to experience one of my frequent attacks. As I fell to the floor in my room and I yelled for help, the pain was becoming overwhelming. There was nothing I could do, but wait for the attack to pass. During each onset of an infection, I felt very tight, hard cramps in my side and lower left back. Often the pain was so bad I would actually pass out. I blacked out for a moment and then I remember my mom yelling to my brother to bring me water while she waited by my side. So my brother, Mark, being the rescuer that he is, ran downstairs and filled a 64 ounce pitcher with water. To this day I remember the look on his face – he wanted to save me – he loved me. In that moment, despite deep pain, I began to smile. He made me laugh as he carried an enormous pitcher of water to my rescue. After that experience I began to realize that no matter what life hands you, you must choose to surround yourself with people who love you.

By the same token, as a young child I learned about feeling like a failure just as much as I learned about being loved. While my family was extremely supportive, there were doctors and even young friends who were not. Each of my experiences, both positive and negative, shaped my beliefs about myself.

The first time I remember feeling insecure about having kidney disease was when I was eleven years old. For a while the kidney infections had stopped and many doctors began to believe I would outgrow the attacks – almost as if my body would adjust to living with the deformed kidney. They even thought I would eventually be fine without further treatment. But when I was 11 years old, my kidney infections started again and became more frequent than ever. Once again, my parents began to seek answers.

It seemed like a million tests were done and nothing was decided. I remember one doctor telling my mom that nothing was wrong with the kidney – as if I had made it all up. After all of the love my parents offered me, it took one person who didn't believe me to change my image of myself. Here I was a young girl who had fought these attacks for so long. But now, I was left to feel vulnerable and often different from my peers. What I needed the most was to feel that I was not at fault for the kidney disease, but somehow I began to think that I was.

Over time, I began to lose my self-confidence. I knew there was something wrong, but according to this doctor I was fine. I remember quietly questioning myself.

Am I making this up? Am I exaggerating?

For a while, as my parents sought answers, I stopped believing in myself. Although I knew something was wrong, I was embarrassed to be me. Why had I let one negative opinion and a few innocent comments, define my feelings about who I was? It would take me years to understand the thoughts I carried as a young child.

Being the fighter that my mom is, she began to fight for me. She fought until someone would listen. So many trips to seek different opinions and many lunch dates with my mom along the way, led us to an amazing doctor at Children's Hospital in Washington, DC. He was an expert in the field of nephrology. The doctor and his team were able to use a new procedure at Children's Hospital which revealed the root of my painful attacks.

"This kidney is dying; it is no longer working," he explained. "Its function is no more than 5 percent. If we don't remove it soon, it will cause your daughter to have a stroke or even a heart attack. Her body cannot live with this kidney," he firmly told my mother.

I felt relieved in a weird way – knowing that this bad news meant that I wasn't lying after all. Somehow the diagnosis made me feel better. My voice was finally heard.

My mom and I knew that we needed to call my father right away to let him know about the doctor's plan for surgery. Looking back, I can see the purple flowers in the carefully manicured lawn outside of the doctor's office.

I can still place myself in that moment so many years ago. My mom spoke to my dad first and then gave the phone to me. He sounded startled. I could tell he'd been crying. I had never known my dad to cry about anything before. I felt strong, even though I was scared, because I somehow knew that I could handle what was ahead.

I reassured him that I was feeling fine about having surgery and I wasn't scared. I focused on the purple flowers to hold back my own tears and provide strength to the two people who loved me the most.

As planned, on May 11, 1987, I had my left kidney removed. Heading to the hospital that morning, I was calm and rested. My brothers walked me arm and arm into the hospital being true examples of love in my life. I remember waking up and feeling nauseous, and then throwing up from the anesthesia, nevertheless I felt loved and that was all I needed.

Often I think about how different my life would be today if I had not had such caring parents. Without my personal suffering, I may have never drawn close enough to my parents to feel their love so deeply. In many ways, I'm grateful to have experienced kidney disease as a child.

As an adult, I realize now that my parents' love for me is a lot like the love I experience in knowing God. It's unconditional, pure, and forgiving. I knew then how wonderful my parents were, but I understand it even more now that I am raising my own daughters.

At the time, my spirituality was not something I was mature enough to understand or recognize. Looking back, I know for sure that my past shaped a lot about what I thought of myself and the world around me. As a child, I was building my spiritual layers without even knowing it.

I think of this time in my life as the point *before* I began searching. I didn't fully understand my relationship with God, but I was being shaped by positive and negative influences. Those influences became more significant later in life as I built my spiritual cake.

As a young fifth grader, I was embarrassed to return to school after my surgery, although most of my friends and teachers were supportive. There was one girl who made fun of me, drew negative attention to me about my surgery, and left me feeling terrible. I wanted to befriend her; to make friends with the enemy and earn her love. She was probably so jealous of the attention that I received after the surgery, but I was too young to understand that type of psychology. I felt rejected by her and, to me, that outweighed all of the support from those who loved me.

I despised her for the way she made me feel. I felt different around her – she was such a bully. As a school teacher today, I can truly appreciate how students feel when they experience bullying. It's difficult to forget that awful fifth grade year.

I allowed her to crush my soul – after all my parents had done to protect me. At the same time, I learned to hide my feelings and remain positive on the outside so no one would see how she affected me. I think about her from time to time and wonder where she is or if she even realizes what she did.

Mostly I would love to know that she has a lot of wrinkles and horrible acne! All kidding aside, I forgave her a long time ago and just hope that someone taught her how to be kind.

As an adult, I realize that we often focus on that one negative comment or interaction while there may be 10 other positive people supporting us. I try very hard to redirect my thoughts to embrace and enjoy the positive influences in my life instead of letting one person destroy my positive self-image. I also realize now that in life there will always be negative people, but each day I release my need to please the negative people and, instead, give more of myself to those who deserve it.

It is true that at every phase of my spiritual growth, love has been a necessary ingredient in my cake. It was my family's love for me that helped me form love for other people. I have learned that if you take time to love others then love will be reciprocated to you. I often stop myself in moments when I don't really want to take the time to listen or when I'm feeling too wrapped up in myself and my own needs, to redirect my thoughts. Recognizing that I am selfish, means that I count on God – the voice inside of me – to remind me of the person I want to be. In order to receive the love I need each day of my life, I must be willing to give that back to others – even when it's not always convenient! So there is a voice, a whisper within my spirit, which reminds me to slow down, to listen, and to take time for love.

If it were not for the love of my parents and my brothers, I may not have learned about love at such an early age. And love may not be shown to every person early in life. However, I believe God gives each of us many opportunities to experience love throughout life. You may have to recreate what love means to you or you may have to redesign relationships to be more authentic, but I promise you that, with love, you will be able to get through anything!

It will take love, even just from one person, to help you build your spiritual self. Each of us deserves authentic love. It is necessary to seek a healthy, loving relationship with someone who reciprocates love to you. It may not be a physical relationship, but we all must start with the belief that we deserve love from a trusted friend.

According to Wikipedia, as an abstract concept, *love* usually refers to a deep, ineffable feeling of tenderly caring for another person. To me, *tenderly caring* are the two most powerful words about love.

It's essential during your crisis that you share your hurts, heartaches, pain, and sadness only with people who are interested enough to be tender to your feelings and caring enough to listen. Not everyone needs to know everything about what you're going through.

Today, I only allow myself to spend time with people who accept me for who I am. At the same time, I try to spend as much time with positive people as I can. I purposefully and politely limit the conversations or time spent with negative people because I've made a choice to share love with others – not negativity.

I've watched marriages fall apart over the absence of tenderly caring behavior. On the other hand, I've witnessed miracles of people who have made it through tremendous storms. Because of love they live stronger and more deeply connected.

Have you ever heard a horrific story, one in which an overwhelming amount of pain or trauma has occurred in someone's life? Of course, we all have. Have you ever wondered how the person who endured so much could even get out of bed or continue to live? I would say it's safe to bet that someone, maybe many people, reached out and offered love during those painful times.

And I am certain that my journey from pain to peace, several layers deep, grew as a result of love. We can all start there and build a better life by focusing first on love.

3

PAIN

*...and everyone believed. They bowed down and worshiped
the LORD because they knew that he had seen their suffering
and was going to help them.*

Exodus 4:31

As a teenager, I was happy. My life was pretty simple. I was
close with my family and had a lot of wonderful friends.
During my junior year, I was dating a college freshman who
had been popular in our high school. I remember how much
I loved the attention he gave me; after all he was a lot older
than anyone I had dated. Many girls in our school were
attracted to him, but he chose me. I felt special and I gained
status by dating him. For me, that was important.

I thought he might have been impressed with my peg-legged
jeans and teased bangs. Maybe it was my overwhelming sense
of style, my red Dodge Daytona, or the way my hair reeked of
Sun-In. Whatever it was, I was proud of myself for attracting
an older man. I made sure my pink lipstick and blue eye
shadow were perfectly placed before seeing him because I was
certain he was *into me!*

Over time, I started to realize that he was not as impressed
with me as I thought. I found out from a few friends that he
was dating other people while dating me. I looked at myself in
the mirror, wondered where I went wrong – maybe my RAVE
hairspray had failed to keep every hair in its perfect place or
maybe my stone washed jeans weren't tight enough - but
nevertheless, I knew I had to stop seeing him.

Finally, on the night I got up the nerve to break up with him, he sexually assaulted me. I was shocked. Things like this didn't happen to small-town girls like me. My group of friends spent the weekends at bonfires and took risks by driving four-wheelers in our friends' backyards. Assault only occurred between boys, drunk off of *Milwaukee's Best*, who were fighting over who owned a better pick-up truck. We were pretty innocent, wildly stupid, but not raised in an abusive culture.

But that night a part of my country-girl innocence was taken away from me. He was never forceful before, but when I asked him to stop, he didn't. He had a hold on me – forcing me to do things that made me feel ashamed. I don't know how long it took me to pull away from the grip he had on my head. Finally, I ran away from him. I was lucky that my girlfriend was in a room nearby and I wasn't alone.

I remember crying to my girlfriend feeling confused by what had happened. I was thankful she was there and that he didn't rape me. The next morning I told my mom everything and a weight was lifted as I cried through every detail. I begged her to keep this a secret as I felt shamed and disgusted.

Immediately my attitude changed. I was sad and depressed and somehow I felt responsible for the attack. At the same time, I kept telling myself to get over it – that things could've been worse. But I couldn't. I was once a happy, carefree teenager and now I was terrified to go anywhere. It was one of the worst feelings I had ever felt. Fear, anxiety, and self-doubt quickly overwhelmed me.

I stayed close to my mom during this period. On Friday nights, we'd watch television and eat pizza in bed. I was taking a strong liking to the show *Picket Fences* and homemade pizza. I wasn't as carefree as I'd once been and my confidence was lost. I felt safe with my mom and more than anything I needed to feel safe.

My fear led me to search for something – anything. Was I looking for God? Where was God? *If I find Him, can He help me heal?* I began to wonder.

My self-esteem was so low and I felt so much shame over what had happened. It had been a long time since I prayed and I felt awkward searching for God. With anxiety, I slowly opened up and decided to ask God to help me. It was time to have a conversation with Him.

I prayed, "God, I need you. I'm so sad. I just want to find a way to feel better about myself. Help me discover the root of my shame. Help me understand why I feel so responsible. Help me to see that I will be okay. God, I need you to help me because I'm not sure how to help myself."

Shorty after, I experienced a calmness that I hadn't felt in a long time. Just as shame cannot be seen, peace cannot be seen, but I felt it. I can only explain this release of pain by recognizing that nothing on the outside had changed, but everything about my self-image was reshaping and improving.

I knew then that God loved me. But it would take years, more pain, and a lot of suffering for me to learn to fully love myself. I was still searching for me. And when you're still searching for yourself, it's hard to grow deeply into the person God created you to be.

I eventually moved past the assault, but it left mental scars I'd never forget. I continued to search for God well into my early adult life. I felt God's presence many times during those years. He made His presence known through a very painful, broken engagement; my college graduation; falling in love again; getting married; and having children!

I often felt Him during the big stuff, but mostly I was still searching. I loved my life for sure and I had a lot to be happy about, but I was not fully satisfied. Something seemed to be missing. My family and friends were amazing, but I had yet to develop a deeper connection with my spirit.

At 27 years old, I found myself in a situation that I couldn't handle on my own. This marked the beginning of a deeper surrendering to God. My husband, Mark, and I were both teachers and we had just built our dream home. To make ends meet, I tutored three kids two nights a week. We needed the money and I was paid well. Mark and our daughter, Danielle, bonded while I was away so it was a great schedule for us all!

I remember driving down a familiar two-lane road with nothing unusual on my mind. Suddenly, I was spinning.

Was I spinning? Was my car spinning? What's happening?

My mind was racing. I was afraid, but coherent enough to control my car. As the dizziness continued, I slowly turned into a church parking lot not far from home. My right ear felt clogged and I was confused. Abruptly, this feeling invaded me and only slowly did it subside.

I decided it must have been a freak occurrence. But a few days later, another similar event occurred and I knew I had to investigate this. I met with a local Otolaryngologist. She immediately ran tests and it wasn't long before she entered the office with a soft look on her face. "I think you have Meniere's disease," she said gently. I had never heard of Meniere's disease and I wanted information – and fast.

According to *Healthwise*, "Ménière's (pronounced "mun-YAIRZ") disease is a disorder of the inner ear that affects hearing and balance. It causes sudden attacks of vertigo (a spinning sensation), tinnitus (a loud ringing in the ears), and a loss of hearing that may become permanent."

The difficulties of this disease started in my right ear – the same ear that was deformed at birth and had previously led doctors to understanding the seriousness of my kidney defects. As I mentioned before, our kidneys and ears run on the same chromosome and it was my deformed ear that clued doctors in on the problem. Now the same opposing ear was the root of the Meniere's disease.

Imagine two balloons in your ear, one inside of the other. The inner balloon, in my case, would swell and put pressure on the outer balloon. When this happened the nerve that controlled the balance function on the right side of my body was affected and this caused me to feel a spinning and sometimes a flipping sensation. The doctor encouraged me to eat a low-salt diet and take a diuretic to flush out the pressure in my ear.

No big deal. I can certainly handle this.

I remember leaving her office and while waiting for my prescription at our local grocery store, I made myself a fresh salad for lunch thinking that the medication and a healthy, low salt-diet would help me overcome the disease. I was hopeful that a new diet would help me to lose a few pounds anyway!

I had come to the pivotal place that every young woman must face in her late 20s – that with each passing year it becomes harder to keep off those few extra, unwanted pounds! So to me this was a new form of willpower. I figured it was time to trade my chicken nuggets for a fruit and yogurt parfait and make the best of it.

I lived with vertigo for about two years, but the attacks were rare. When Danielle was 20 months, Mark and I welcomed our second baby, Kaitlyn. My pregnancy was considered high risk because I had just one kidney. Of course, I somehow can't seem to take the "normal" route to do anything worthwhile and so at 25 weeks into my pregnancy, I began having contractions. With medication to stop the contractions and bed rest, I made it through and our gorgeous baby girl was born at 34 weeks.

My health was finally under control and I was learning to balance sleepless nights, crying fits, and being a mom of two under two!

But unfortunately within a year after Kaitlyn was born, the attacks began again and were more frequent and violent than before. At this time in my life, I was a stay-at-home mom and had started my own small business to make ends meet. One of the worst attacks occurred at a small business conference I was attending with my mom and several friends. I was excited to be able to enjoy time with adults. While eating lunch that afternoon, I was jolted by a spinning sensation. Everything around me was moving. I hated to embarrass myself in a room full of people so I quietly made my way out of the arena and closer to a quiet corner in the conference hall.

Then the nausea swept through my entire body. What a nightmare. I realized this attack would not be over as easily as it started. Soon I was lying down, exposed, as conference participants left the luncheon, showing my vulnerability to what felt like the world. Closing my eyes as tightly as I could would provide a bit of relief, but the spinning, whirling, and nausea continued to pound me. Hoping my medication would help, my mom held my head as I took a dose.

Any movement caused me to throw up. I threw up eight times that day. With no sign of the attack stopping, a team of paramedics came to move me to a hotel recovery room. Four hours later, the attack subsided. I felt weak, helpless, and really pissed off.

After the conference, the attacks became part of my daily life. Each day I was plagued with thoughts of vertigo. I feared when an attack would invade me and how long it would last. Sometimes they lasted an hour or two, others longer. Each time I was sick and unable to feel comfort, or proceed with life normally, or feel human in any way.

I tried everything – a low-salt diet, caffeine restriction, adding more sleep and less stress to my life, increasing the diuretic I was taking and adding herbal supplements to my diet, and even acupuncture. The acupuncture wasn't even covered by my insurance, but I had to try all potential solutions. My life began to literally spin out of control.

A year later, I was still suffering. One afternoon I was pulling out of the driveway heading to pick up my daughters from preschool when suddenly I began to feel a flipping sensation.

It was as if the car had become an instant upside down roller coaster ride – with no warning.

I screamed wildly and random thoughts raced through my mind. As the car flipped upside down, I wondered when it would stop and how I could prepare for a crash landing. The sensations were so real; I knew for sure I was about to crash.

As the flipping slowed down and the spinning began, that's when it hit me.

Shocked. Enraged. Furious. I was completely fooled by this monster – tricked into thinking my car had failed me and that I was *actually* flipping upside down.

A flush of anger raged through my body. I couldn't even catch my breath – I struggled to make my way inside and immediately phoned my mom.

"I hate this!" I yelled to her. "This is so awful. I can't live like this anymore!" I could no longer remain positive about this horrible disease. I was horrified by what had happened.

With many other disabilities some portion of a normal life can be continued, but vertigo disrupts virtually every aspect of life. The nausea and vomiting combined with the out-of-control spinning sensation often left me totally incapacitated.

My deepest fear was having an attack while in the car with my children. I just couldn't take that risk any longer. On that day, with sadness and resentment, I made the decision to stop driving and start asking for help.

My mother and father eventually moved in with our family to help me raise our children because I could no longer do it on my own. While my husband, Mark, was at work each day I couldn't be left alone with our girls since the attacks were sudden and debilitating.

This was not me! I had always been a very successful, hardworking person. I was once an independent, determined woman. I had dreams about our future as a family. I was willing to work hard to accomplish my goals, but at this point in my life I felt like a loser. I wasn't dependable anymore. Quickly I began to lose myself and doubt my abilities as a mother.

During all of my suffering, I found myself searching *a lot.* I hated the vertigo. I hated my life. I hated everything. I was angry. I didn't deserve to live like a prisoner in my own body. I was so resentful of the people in my life and although they were there to help me, I hated asking for help because I was losing more and more of my independence as each day passed.

I began suffering like never before. Once a happy and outgoing person, I was now depressed and hopeless. I quietly cried to myself as I waited for each attack to pass. As tears suffused my eyes, the pain of this disease filled my soul. I felt as if I had lost it all. I went from being a strong woman, a proud wife and mother, a protector, a nurturer, and a provider to our family to a useless human being.

Just as I learned to hide my pain as a child, feeling embarrassed like a young schoolgirl once again, I hid my pain from most of my family and friends. Asking for help meant I had to admit the severity of my situation and it was terribly difficult for me to face how much I needed people.

My doctor prescribed a steroid to help control the length of the attacks. Prednisone helped the vertigo subside within a few hours, but not without a price. The drug made me jittery and edgy. Most nights I wasn't able to sleep for more than three hours. I spent countless nights on the couch watching late-night television which certainly wasn't productive. But at the time, Prednisone was a better option than nausea and dizziness.

I was hungry all the time because the Prednisone made me ravenous. I needed food and a lot of it. Somehow fruit and yogurt was NOT what I wanted. I stuffed the same amount of food in my 5'3" frame as my 6'1" husband, and still wasn't satisfied.

I despised going into my closet to get dressed. I was swollen, fat, and undesirable. I looked at myself in the mirror and thought, "Who are you?"

I didn't even recognize myself. I wore the same jeans over and over again – mommy jeans that were faded and only acceptable in the first few weeks after giving birth – because that was all I could fit into. Gaining extra weight certainly didn't add to my state of mind. I felt so ugly both inside and out.

I was so angry with God for the way my life had turned out. If He is all love, only kindness, and wants only what is best for me, how could He let this happen? What kind of God would let me suffer this way? I began to question everything I knew about Him.

What I realize today, that I didn't know then, was that my suffering would force me to surrender. I needed God to come into my life and rescue me.

One morning after my mom and I dropped the girls off at preschool, we decided to attend a bible study at our church. Honestly, I don't know why I agreed to go as I never attended a bible study in the past and wasn't sure if it was right for me.

It felt awkward to me – to sit there and talk about something as private as faith – with people I didn't really know. But, I wanted to "test" God to see if He was really there. I had nowhere else to turn. It was a risk I was willing to take – to open myself to God and see if He was really listening. During the study I met women who had fully surrendered their own pain to Jesus Christ. They shared their own stories of moving from pain to peace. Interested *enough* and deeply desperate, I continued to go.

Over time, I saw the power in accepting Him. I knew I had to take responsibility in my own relationship with God.

I needed to go directly to God, to surrender, and ask for help. Just as I felt vulnerable, angry, and afraid that I had to ask for help from my parents, my husband, and my friends, I was afraid to ask for help from God. What if He didn't answer me? Then what? Then, I would have clearly exhausted all of my options. I wasn't sure if God could give me what I needed.

If I was going to feel God's presence I had to change my attitude. I needed to believe that I deserved to be happy again. I had to stop feeling sorry for myself and simply trust God.

I took control of my thoughts – desiring a peaceful life again. In guarding my thoughts, choosing to be positive and seeking love, I knew my life would improve. I was tired of being so angry.

I got on my knees, with the heat of tears on my face, and asked God to help me pick up the broken pieces of my life. I asked Jesus Christ to come into my life again, and to live once more in my heart. I apologized for how ugly I had been, for the horrible thoughts that had consumed my mind. I asked God to show me how I could fight this disease with a positive outlook instead of being so determined to hate it.

I just talked out loud to God (for what seemed like forever) and begged Him for what I needed. I put up no fronts. I talked to Him the way I'd talk to a friend.

In prayer I learned the greatest lesson of my life. God cannot help those who are not willing to help themselves. It was only when I became open and allowed God into my life – into the parts of my life that I hated, into the hurt, into the pain, and into the depression that I began to feel His presence. Almost immediately I began to feel differently about God, myself, and the vertigo.

Finally, I learned to surrender. Once broken, crushed, and changed by something that I couldn't control, I surrendered my pain to God because I wanted to be happy again.

I felt a glimmer of hope about my life and was beginning to feel like myself again! I truly believe it was only because I was open to Him and I desired a personal relationship with Jesus. He could only be there for me if I was willing to let Him.

We had to build a relationship together. Building a relationship with Him meant that I had to be open to the lessons He was teaching me. I had to understand the truth about Him. I decided to trust Him and prayed that He'd never leave me.

Almost immediately, I began experiencing peace in a way that I never imagined. I thought it would be so difficult to find God. I thought He had not been present in my pain and that turning to Him would be daunting. Instead, I learned that there is an unspeakable peace that can live in one's soul. A peace that is so pure, so comforting, that it can only be explained by knowing God.

By getting on my knees and asking for help, I realized that the peace I was experiencing was coming from reestablishing my relationship with the Lord.

I believe that being "saved" is not just about eternal life. I wanted and needed to be saved on Earth; saved each day from the evil thoughts, the hatred, and the pain in my life. I began to look at my life differently – through God's eyes.

My spirituality was growing layer by layer. I was still experiencing the vertigo, but my spirit was changing.

My relationship with God became the greatest gift that resulted from my vertigo. In knowing God, I discovered that my vertigo had a purpose, that my illness could not take away my soul, and that it was a gift to know when and how to ask for help.

As time passed I learned to be less angry and more willing to ask for what I needed. I learned to embrace the fact that people wanted to help me and that if I let them it was better for them and for me.

I knew I could dig myself into another deep, dark hole and just live there or I could choose a path of perseverance. Instead, I explored available surgical options and was willing to see God's light. I learned how to walk in faith instead of fear and was willing to embrace the journey. I chose to give up some of the things I couldn't control and learned to change the things I could. Of course I couldn't change my deformed ear or the vertigo, but I could control how I'd react to this disease.

Physically, after years of dealing with the attacks and thinking my only option was to remain on steroids to control the vertigo, I opened my eyes to other medical options.

Spiritually, I opened my eyes to God and exposed myself layer by layer. I didn't know it at the time, but God was using my raw, inner-most thoughts to move me closer to the person I was meant to be.

When I look into the eyes of others, I wonder where they are in building their spiritual cake. For some people, it takes years to move out of searching and suffering. I understand how hard it is to surrender and trust God completely. I feel blessed in some ways to have endured so much suffering because my experiences helped me understand God's love for me.

4

FAITH

And this hope is what saves us. But if we already have what we hope for, there is no need to keep on hoping. However, we hope for something we have not yet seen, and we patiently wait for it. In certain ways we are weak, but the Spirit is here to help us. For example, when we don't know what to pray for, the Spirit prays for us in ways that cannot be put into words.

Romans 8:24-26

What I learned during the most difficult days of my life is that God does not allow us to suffer from kidney disease, vertigo, cancer, or any other illness without a reason. And when I was ready, I found God waiting for me with open arms, ready to love and accept me just the way I was - imperfect.

I think about the love I have for my own children. I am reminded of how much I want them to succeed, be healthy, and feel happy and complete. God is our heavenly father - our creator. Just as I would never wish harm, sadness, or tragedy on my own children, God, our father, never allows us to suffer without reason.

I know God is love. Just the way I feel love for my daughters, God has a love for me that is unconditional and pure. He never punishes me for doing wrong, but instead offers forgiveness for the times I fail. I know my pain was a result of pulling away from God and not allowing Him into my life sooner. I am positive, by my own experience, that God only wants what is best for me - always. He wants what's best for all of His children, including you!

Knowing that God only wants what's best for His children brought me comfort through my vertigo. I began to feel a spirit of hope and I was certain my pain was over. I quickly learned that was not the case. I would endure more heartache and suffering, but now I could handle things differently than before. Now I had hope.

So after careful consideration, I chose to have a surgery called a vestibular nerve section. The purpose was to clip the nerve that controlled the balance function on my right side. By blocking that nerve, my brain would learn to compensate and become controlled by the entire left side of my body. Through rehabilitation and a long recovery, I would learn to walk again and regain all balance function because the left side of my brain would learn to take over for the offending side. It was a big deal to elect to have a surgery like this, but I felt desperate. The success rate in stopping the vertigo was 97 percent and I was thrilled by those odds.

The surgery involved opening the Dura – the lower part of my brain. By this point in my life, I had been through so much that the thought of brain surgery really wasn't that scary! I was excited to get my life back – possibly without vertigo.

In September of 2006, I went to the hospital to have the vestibular nerve section. Before the surgery began, a spinal drain was inserted into my back. A Lumbar Cerebrospinal Fluid (CSF) drain is often used during neurosurgery to relax the brain, and improve the doctor's ability to see inside of the brain. As the medical team prepared all around me, something unexpected happened. The computer system, that monitored several different nerves, crashed. This meant that the surgeon could not track the function of specific nerves which control hearing, balance and more. Never in 20 years had the doctor ever experienced something similar. Because the entire system crashed, the surgery quickly ended.

I woke up feeling sore, but took the news well. I went into this surgery expecting the best and ended up without the results I was expecting. Through my disappointment, I did feel a presence of peace. God was there and He was revealing a greater plan to me. I held on to the idea of having the surgery and talked that day with the doctor about rescheduling.

As that day progressed, I became very sore. Soon my back and neck felt stiff and it was difficult to walk. I did not have surgery so why was I feeling so bad? Maybe it was the anesthesia, but I wasn't even strong enough to change my own shirt. That evening, I slept and hoped to feel better in the morning.

The next two days were awful. I was in so much pain whenever I tried to pick up my head. My only relief was when I laid completely still. Once again, I found myself needing help. My mom spoon-fed me, Mark completely took over with the kids, and my dad helped in any way he could.

The pain didn't make sense. After the third day, Mark took me to the emergency room where I was given a ton of pain medication and told to go back home. I sincerely think the doctors in the ER must have thought I was overreacting. I never had surgery! *Truly, what could be wrong with me?* We waited in the ER for hours, but to no avail. The doctors didn't try to figure out the root of my pain. They just filled me with drugs! Doctors came in and out, but I felt like a nuisance – not a priority on their caseload for the evening.

I remember receiving several shots of pain medication and feeling completely doped. Mark and I look back today at my behavior in the ER only to laugh at how ridiculous I acted. I was so drugged! I waved at people, talked to myself, and told some very strange stories. My speech was slurred and I was feeling happy for the moment – intoxicated, but happy.

Apparently I was making friends with other crazy people in the ER, pretending that I knew them and that they were interested in talking to me. I'm sure Mark wanted to leave me there with the other nutcases to let me finish my drug-induced party! But Mark is an awesome husband and took my pain seriously. He continued to seek answers. We waited through the night and with enough pain medication in my system to tell the nurses I was feeling better, I was sent home to rest.

The next day brought nothing more than irrational pain. My head and neck were stiff and I was unable to move. It wasn't until a friend recognized my symptoms that we began to realize what was happening. She had faced a similar type of pain after a spinal tap during childbirth. The way she described her experience gave us hope that there may be something similar happening to me. We learned that neurological injury caused by needle insertion causes chronic head and neck pain. It became clear that I was experiencing a CSF leak.

Finally, I went back to the emergency room with my own small army of support! My family demanded a spinal patch which is a quick procedure. Blood is taken from your arm and shot into your back allowing the blood to act as a patch to the leak. Within thirty minutes I was feeling relief and it was obvious that this procedure could have been done five days earlier. As suspected, the leak occurred because the needle inserted in my back prior to surgery was mismarked and my spinal sack had been punctured.

Had my doctor picked up on this sooner I could have avoided all unnecessary suffering. I learned later that he had endured his own crisis. During my painful ordeal at home, my doctor's father-in-law had a heart attack in front of his entire family and died soon after. I was sympathetic to his situation and knew I needed to forgive him. I had to make peace with my pain by forgiving my doctor's inattentiveness to me. Without forgiving him, I couldn't move forward. His mistake, although a huge mistake to let a patient suffer unnecessarily, was not intentional and deserved forgiveness.

Besides, I couldn't lose my faith now – just because things had been difficult. Although I experienced an awful result from the first attempt at surgery, I knew I needed God in order to remain strong. Heading down a path of depression, negativity, and heartache was an option - but not an option I was willing to explore anymore.

I continued to surrender, trust God, and recognize what was out of my control.

I prayed and felt God directing me to attempt the surgery again. It was still the only option that would provide a 97 percent chance of living without vertigo - and the goal had not changed.

In October of the same year, we attempted the surgery a second time. Of course, the spinal drain was a huge concern. My doctor knew that my spine was prone to a leak and further preparation was necessary. So, I arrived at the hospital the night before to ensure the drain was placed properly this time. I felt confident.

Finally, I woke from the surgery I so desperately wanted - a surgery that would leave me feeling worse before I got better - but would ultimately give me my life back.

Again, the surgery failed. This time, the bone around my ear was cut, my brain was open and the surgeon was ready, but the nerve to be cut was wrapped in blood vessels - so many blood vessels that clipping the nerve could cause me to bleed to death. Cutting the nerve was no longer an option. I became the second patient of my doctor's twenty year career who had a nerve that presented itself this way.

He knew how long I had suffered with vertigo and wanted to at least try an option that would help me live with fewer attacks. Therefore, he inserted shunts into my ear. Shunts are designed to drain excess fluid from the ear and carry it to other parts of the body. According to Wikipedia, "This valve usually sits outside the skull, but beneath the skin, somewhere behind the ear." And although the use of shunts and their reliability are questionable, it was the only option I had at the time. I awoke feeling disappointed, but I believed that God would see me through once again.

I trusted that He was there during the surgery and that I would see the big picture, a reason, one day. I never expected God to reveal the answers to me in this lifetime, but I did trust His plan and I was willing to be faithful. In being faithful I believe that everything does happen for a reason, and I felt peace about the results once again.

Without prayer, I may not have survived the next series of events, but luckily I found God earlier in my journey. Several hours after surgery, I found myself doubled over in pain once again – only this time it was worse. The sharp, stabbing pain ran from my head to my toes, through my back and down my legs, up my arms, and into my neck. I don't know how I remained peaceful, but I learned that I had a strength within myself that was much greater than I ever knew. Somehow I knew I would get through this.

However, by the second day of the excruciating pain, I couldn't take it anymore. I felt like I'd been sliced open. I felt as if my back had been beaten with a hammer and my neck was broken into a million little pieces. Still, within my soul there was a peaceful hope that I would somehow find relief.

During this time of suffering I instantly surrendered my pain to God. My faith was running several layers deep – from searching to suffering to surrendering – once again.

Mark called an ambulance to take me to the emergency room knowing that he couldn't transfer me in a car. The thought of riding upright in a car to the hospital was more than I could handle. When we finally arrived in the emergency room, I begged for pain medication which was quickly administered. An angel must have been sent to care for me that evening. I don't know his name, but he believed in me and was willing to help. Heavy doses of drugs were injected into me; any drug to try and alleviate my pain. But there was no relief in sight.

An MRI would later determine the cause of my horrifying pain. I clearly remember what it felt like to lie still for that MRI. A cold, hard table. A vacant stillness. Insurmountable, unexplainable pain. Heavy tears streamed down my face. My eyes were swollen and stung from crying so much. Yet, I needed this test and had to remain strong in order to get through.

I looked to God for comfort and repeated Philippians 4:13 – "I can do all things through Christ who strengthens me." Somewhere deep in my soul I knew I would be fine. After the MRI, I was admitted to the hospital...and left to wait.

As Mark and my mom stood by my side, the pressure to find answers began to take a toll on them. More than anything else they wanted to support me, but they were growing deeply frustrated with slow answers and dead ends.

As I looked at Mark and noticed the tears in his eyes, I couldn't help but think back to our beginning. Life was so simple then; much different from where life had us at the moment.

I flashed back to the night we met and smiled quietly to myself. I remembered it like it was yesterday. We noticed each other, shared a few *Miller Lites*, and connected instantly. I saw in him what I had been looking for – someone who could really make me laugh. He saw in me a woman who loved sports, (which was actually a lie I told him in order to make a good first impression) but regardless we both quickly knew that we had a future together. He likes to tell people that we met in a bar, I was drunk, and he took me home! Despite his humor, I look back on that evening now and smile. Never in a million years would I have known then just how much I would need him to make me laugh in order to handle our pain.

But now, I struggled to even lie in bed because no matter what I did, I was unable to feel relief. The pain compounded and with each passing hour I asked myself how I'd survive this nightmare. Conversely, somewhere deep inside of me was the reminder that I was going to be okay. This gave me hope when hope was hard to find.

I vaguely remember an elderly woman who came into my room to offer me the Eucharist. The Eucharist, often called Holy Communion, is a Christian Sacrament honoring the life, suffering, death, and resurrection of Jesus. To me, the Eucharist is a source of hope.

"Something good will come out of this," the elderly woman said. I'm not sure why I believed her, but I did. As I waited for someone to read the results of the MRI, nurses filled me with more pain medication and valium to keep me comatose.

Several layers underneath my pain, was peace within my soul that reminded me I was not alone.

After suffering gravely for three solid days, the chief of neurosurgery read my MRI and discovered the nerves in my spinal sack were inflamed. These inflamed nerves were the root of my awful pain. Once again, the spinal drain caused horrible complications involving my spinal sack.

My entire central nervous system was under attack. After several shots of Prednisone - the same Prednisone I took to control the vertigo - I felt better. Slowly I recovered and was able to live pain free with only the memories of that terrible experience.

Now a new light was shining over me. Hope was living within my soul. I never felt alone during that experience. It was a sense of peace, so deep, beyond the pain that allowed me to truly feel God's presence during my darkest moments and I wanted nothing more than to move forward with a spirit of hope for my future.

Vertigo is still a part of my life today, but not at all like it was when I lost my freedom to drive, live comfortably, and function. I will never be cured of Meniere's disease, but with faith I am certain I'll make it through life knowing that God is watching over me. The vertigo did improve as a result of having the shunts placed in my ear, but I believe deep in my soul that it was God who healed me. I have no doubt that I would have not been strong enough to face the pain, the failed surgeries, and the disappointments without Him.

Today my ability to hear in my right ear fluctuates quite a bit. Some days I can't hear out of it at all, which is a normal side effect of Meniere's disease. I find it annoying when I can't hear someone, but mostly I just have to laugh at myself. My family and friends tease me when I answer them with an odd response because I didn't hear the question correctly! I would consider a hearing aid, but insurance just doesn't cover it. That seems insane to me!

All of these experiences led me to think a lot about faith. What is faith really? I never claim to have all of the answers, but I can speak to my own experience - I found faith as my primary source of comfort during my most awful days.

To me, faith is about surrendering your life to God. It's about being able to trust Him when you don't want to or it seems impossible. Faith is about believing the truth about God. God is love. He is only love and never harmful or hurtful.

Our world is full of pain and God certainly doesn't promise a life without it. We live on this earth with our worldly minds, hateful people, devastating disease, and unavoidable tragedy. God is not the root of this pain - He is not the cause. He wants to save us, His children, by providing peace and comfort while we live on earth. But God also has a plan that prepares us for eternal life - sometimes this plan includes suffering.

Our lives are merely a blink in time. It is in our eternal life where we'll experience divine peace, joy, and constant love. We must work with God to survive life on earth so that one day we can enjoy the benefits of eternal life.

People from around the world will argue different viewpoints about religion and faith. I don't choose to argue. My faith is simple. I trust God, I embrace His unconditional love for me, and I ask Him to help me fight all evil in this world. I want to serve God by giving my best to others. To me, faith is asking for the strength to think less about myself and more about helping others. I pray that He will help me stay focused on positive thoughts about myself, my skills, my talents, and my inner beauty so that I can respect Him by loving myself. Another part of my faith is trusting God in every situation – surrendering to Him.

One gift that came along with vertigo is realizing that I'm still strong and powerful, yet I do need help from time to time – just like all of us! There's no shame in admitting you don't have all of the answers or that you need other people. Certainly a powerful gift was getting to know God for all He is and all He is willing to be – you just have to ask for His help.

I learned about undying hope and remaining faithful during joyful and difficult times in my life. After recovering from both surgeries and the awful complications from each, I felt unstoppable. I had a new respect for life and my health. This new found respect would prepare me to face an even tougher battle – one I could never have imagined.

5

CHAOS

We know that God is always at work for the good of everyone who loves him. They are the ones God has chosen for His purpose.

Romans 8:28

It is proven that the part of our brain which registers emotion is the strongest. That is why we can clearly recall how we felt in a situation, feel the emotions over and over again, but can't remember what we ate for breakfast yesterday. It's the emotional side that takes over in important situations.

I have many beautiful memories of my wedding, but there was one significant moment right after the ceremony when my new husband and I were in the limo alone for the first time as husband and wife. I remember feeling ecstatic about the commitment I had just made. I can literally pull those feelings out again! I don't know what we said to each other, but I will never forget the feeling I had at that significant moment.

The emotional side of the brain also carries the burden of tragic memories. I'm sure you can remember where you were on September 11, 2001. The devastating attack on our country was horrific. I was teaching 4th grade at Rock Creek Valley Elementary in Maryland – an average, All-American school. My principal, whom I adored, stood at my classroom door and waved me over towards him.

"Two planes have crashed into the World Trade Center. We will be dismissing early today," he whispered to me. I was dumbfounded. Seriously, what was he talking about? Having no way to turn on a television and only a very small amount of information to dissect, I was confused. The shear confusion is probably something with which we can all relate. I walked through most of that day stunned. With each attack shown repeatedly on television, I cried and was heartsick for my country and those directly affected.

Like all Americans, we recognized the sheer evil, horror, and sadness of that day. I sobbed and felt lost – how could this happen in America? I anxiously called my father who was working in Washington, DC and choked back tears when he confirmed he was safe. I knew there were others who weren't so lucky and I wept for those families who would endure so much pain.

I began searching – wondering where God could be during this terrible nightmare. We were all searching and suffering.

As a country, we were devastated but showed pride in a new way. Within days, most every American wore a pin, displayed a banner, and hung a flag to show unity. We truly became one. In my lifetime I have never seen such love for our country so proudly displayed by Americans. We reached out and stood as one.

I wish the people of this country were as unified and tolerant of each other today as we were after being attacked. As horrific as September 11th and its aftermath was, the unity and love among our people was overwhelming. To me, that love is a reflection of God. I believe when we support each other, show love to strangers, and unite during hardship, we are expressing ourselves the way God intended.

Just as Americans united after the devastating attacks on our country, we rally around each other when a loved one is attacked by disease.

Cancer has a way of showing itself just like 9/11 – sneaking up without warning only to cause devastation in its wake. It's the horrifying news, the confusion, the fear, and the way we unite when someone is newly diagnosed with illness that reminds me of other tragic times in our nation's history.

In that moment of horror, after being diagnosed, people are most giving, most loving, and most united. So why does it take tragedy to bring people together? Wouldn't we all be better off if we acted with a sense of unity, love, and hope all the time? I would soon discover what it was like to be the recipient of unconditional generosity, love, and unity. And it all started with an annoying little pimple – a bump on my face that would change everything.

For about three months I had a bump on my face that wouldn't go away.

Everyone in my family noticed the spot and began to ask me about it.

"I guess it's just a big pimple – I don't know," I'd respond. I stood in front of the mirror many nights trying different anti-pimple creams and wondering why it wouldn't go away.

My brother found humor in pointing out my large facial blemish.

With a smile on his face, my oldest brother, Mike, joked with me. "What the hell is that thing?" he teased.

As the youngest child in our family, I gave in to the teasing. We both laughed. I told him he was just jealous since I don't normally get pimples!

"Goodness, that thing is disgusting," he joked sarcastically. "Good thing you're not dating!"

I was a grown woman, but to him, I was his little sister – someone he could tease as usual.

"Thanks Mike. You look great, too," I poked back.

Amid the teasing, Mike's face became sullen. I could tell he was concerned. "You should get that looked at," he managed with a smile.

"I will," I said. Of course, I wasn't worried.

For the first time in my life I made an appointment to see a dermatologist.

"It's only a cyst," the dermatologist told me. After an injection of cortisone and a week of tetracycline, the *cyst* was not shrinking. I went back to finally have the *cyst* surgically removed. "You will have a tiny scar," I remember the doctor explaining. During a quick procedure, the spot was removed and then sent off to pathology for a routine biopsy.

On the morning I returned to the office to have the stitches removed I was carefree and calm. My kids were off to preschool and I felt excited about the freedom I had – for a few short hours. If you are a parent, you know what I'm talking about. Raising young children is difficult and breaks are appreciated; even though my break included a doctor's visit.

The surgeon greeted me with a small smile and talked calmly while removing my stitches. "The biopsy revealed that what we removed was more than a cyst. We really need to confirm the diagnosis," he shared with limited details.

"No problem," I replied cheerfully. I kept thinking *I feel fantastic – nothing could be wrong!* I felt untouchable. The surgeon mentioned the area may need a little more attention – a deeper removal of tissue. But I wasn't bothered. Certainly a little scraping of a minor bump wouldn't be a problem.

I asked the nurse, at the end of the appointment, if she would write down the name of the possible diagnosis so that I would be knowledgeable when the doctor called to confirm the results.

"No," she said. She explained that they didn't want me to worry and start reading all kinds of information on the internet that later might mean nothing to me anyway. I agreed. Looking back, I was so naive.

What I didn't realize was that the doctors and nurses were actually in shock. They could not believe the pathology report and they wanted the test run again. So I waited.

It was February 26th, 2007 - my 31st Birthday. My young daughters and I celebrated with a kid-friendly lunch and I couldn't wait for Mark to get home from work. I don't remember our plans for the evening because at 3:13 p.m., I received a phone call that changed my life forever - it definitely shattered any birthday plans we had.

With a rattle in her voice, the nurse said, "Meredith, we received the pathology report and we need you to come in tomorrow."

"Why?" I asked.

"You have Merkel Cell Carcinoma (MCC). It's cancer."

With a disbelief in the seriousness of the situation I asked for the spelling, wrote the name quickly, and with hope, hung up the phone.

Similar to the confusion I felt on September 11th, being diagnosed with cancer left me feeling as if I was in a fog. Quickly I searched the internet to learn more about Merkel Cell Carcinoma - a cancer that I didn't even know existed.

Merkel Cell, I read, is a very aggressive and rare form of cancer.

According to Pathology and Laboratory Medicine (2003), "Merkel cell carcinoma (MCC) is an uncommon, highly aggressive cutaneous neoplasm of neuroendocrine. Differentiation with a poor prognosis. MCC most often presents as a painless, firm, raised lesion in sun-exposed sites of the head and neck region of the elderly. The overall one and two-year survival rates were 80 and 53 percent, respectively."

My eyes quickly saw the words: highly aggressive, poor prognosis, and only a 53 percent survival rate, as if they were the only words on the page. At that moment, it was as if they were in bold print shouting out to me, YOU MIGHT DIE!

It's quite possible that this cancer will kill me within two years.

Panic set in. *Oh my God. I'm dying of cancer. How can this be? How can I die at such a young age? I don't want to die.*

There was no bold print on the screen that day. In fact, there was actually other information that offered a glimmer of hope. But in that moment, I crumbled. I was lost, devastated, confused, and unsure of what to do next. So I kept searching. I wanted to find the right information.

My heart was pounding, my hands were shaking, and I needed answers. Each website offered similar information: aggressive, rare, elderly, sun-exposed, and none of it made sense. *This has to be a mistake! It can't really be happening. I'm not old enough for this. I hate lying out in the sun. I feel fantastic. I'm not sick. I CANNOT HAVE CANCER!*

After reading for what felt like an eternity, I decided to call my brother, Mark. He was strong. He would tell me I was going to be okay. Of course he wouldn't cry in front of me, I thought, so I called him first.

"Mark, I have to talk to you." My voice was shaky and my palms were sweaty. My heart was racing so fast and I was nervous.

This was the first time I had to say the words, "I have cancer" out loud. "I had something removed off of my face that was supposed to be a cyst and it turned out to be a tumor. It's called Merkel Cell Carcinoma," I explained.

"Well I'm sure it will be okay. What is that?" Mark quickly wanted an explanation.

As I expected, he was calm, although I know today that at that moment he was crying inside. He asked a lot of questions and listening to myself give him answers terrified me.

It was the meek survival rates that frightened me. It was the fact that I didn't know if the cancer had spread and I could not understand how I could feel so healthy and have cancer. I had been through so much in my life. Certainly I didn't deserve to be dealt this hand.

I paced the floor as I read statistics and facts to him. With each breath I took, I found it harder to breathe.

I grabbed the hair on top of my head and felt myself becoming an emotional wreck. While still holding my head in one hand, I fell to the floor. I sobbed as I lay in the corner of our home office with the phone up to one ear and a pain in my heart so deep I felt paralyzed.

In that moment, all Mark could say was "Mere, it's going to be okay. Mere, I know you are going to be okay. Mere, Mere, I love you."

I don't remember how much time passed before I hung up the phone, but as I lay on the floor soaked from the tears that were pouring down my face, I wanted nothing more than to dig a hole for myself and hide. After all I had just been through, this felt so unfair. Dying was a welcomed option at that moment.

As I lay in my own pile of tears having the biggest pity party of my life, I know for sure that there was a voice whispering calmly in my ear, "Meredith, get up. You can get up. You have to get up."

Above all, the deep pain I had experienced earlier in life somehow prepared me for what I had to face. It was a moment in which God took over and began to guide me through this journey. I had a choice. I could continue to feel sorry for myself. I had absolutely every right to be angry, pissed off, let down, sad, and weak, but I also had a choice to listen to the voice that spoke to me – to surrender to God and let Him be my co-pilot.

I believe that it was the Holy Spirit living within me – that can only be fully awakened by knowing Jesus – that spoke to me that day. I knew then that God was with me and that I would have to surrender my fears to Him once again.

And so I did. By some miracle, with a force greater than myself, I stood on my own two feet again. I was afraid, but ready to fight. I swear it was from that moment on that I decided to fight with a positive outlook.

I chose to stand tall because I knew everyone else around me was about to fall down.

My husband, Mark, came home from work that day and as I began to explain *the phone call* and rattled off *the diagnosis* he asked, "Is that serious?"

"Yes it is and I am so sorry." I began to cry, but only a little. I felt as if apologizing would make things better. Somehow I wanted to convey that I was sorry for the pain I knew he would endure because of my cancer. I wanted to take it all away from him because I knew that I'd be okay. I just wasn't sure about him.

By now my daughters had set up a game of Candy Land and they had no idea anything was wrong. As I spent time with our girls, only 2 and 4 years old at the time, Mark raced to the computer to learn more about a cancer that might just kill his wife.

When he came back, his eyes were red. He'd been crying. "I cannot believe this. This is so unfair." He was angry. "I have got to get out of here," he said as his eyes filled with tears. I actually could understand why he wanted to leave. He couldn't face me while he fell apart.

I got up from the game and walked with him toward the door – stopping him before he left. I needed to hold him; to be there for him.

"Don't you dare die on me. Promise me you won't die." Tears slowly streamed down his face. I had never really seen him cry like that before. He looked pale. His tone was aggressive as if he meant for me to make a truthful promise. I was calm.

"You are my best friend in the whole world Mark, I won't leave you."

"Please promise me." It was as if he thought I could control the outcome. He needed me to be responsible in that moment. I would tell him what he needed to hear and I needed to hear it, too.

"I promise," I said. And he left.

As my family crumbled around me at the thought of facing my cancer, I continued to play Candy Land and began to pray.

6

ACCEPTANCE

*If you are tired from carrying heavy burdens, come to me and
I will give you rest. Take the yoke I give you. Put it on your
shoulders and learn from me. I am gentle and humble, and
you will find rest. This yoke is easy to bear, and this burden is
light.*

Matthew 11:28-30

In an instant, everything can change. For me, it was one
phone call and the words, "You have cancer," that would
change my life forever.

With grim survival rates and what felt like a deadly diagnosis, I
was scared indeed; unsure of why I had to endure more pain
after all I'd just been through. It just didn't seem fair.

To be honest, it was the *waiting* that was the most difficult part
of my journey. There was just so much time passing, so much
waiting, and so much that I didn't know and would not be
able to have answers to right away. My eyes sting with tears
today as I look back and realize how difficult it was to wait
peacefully.

As Mark and I drove to meet the Head and Neck Surgeon at
Johns Hopkins hospital, I felt hopeful that he would have the
answers to our many questions. Since we live about an hour
from Baltimore, we felt blessed to be so close to such a world-
renowned hospital. But Merkel Cell was a stranger to most,
almost unheard of in a 31-year-old woman, and it was no
surprise when I learned that I was one of few Merkel Cell
patients to be treated at Hopkins.

On the ride to the appointment Mark and I went over our questions, once again, to make sure we would leave nothing out. My parents waited anxiously by the phone knowing that we would call as soon as we left the office. Many friends called on the morning of the appointment to offer encouragement and love. I felt strong. I was ready to hear what the doctor had to say. So I thought.

We got off of the elevator on the 8th floor where the sign read, "Head and Neck Cancer." *That sign is for me*, I thought to myself privately. *That's what I have. Take a deep breath...deep breath.* I breathed in and felt the tears building inside me, ready to come pouring out at any moment. I squeezed them back because I was prepared to be strong for Mark and me.

We met the doctor, who was nice, but not exactly the most compassionate man. He did what I needed him to do – give me the facts without sugar-coating the diagnosis.

"Merkel Cell is not a cancer we can take chances with," he told us firmly. Then he outlined "the plan" and offered no choices because with Merkel Cell there weren't any. I sat there with a notepad writing down everything he told us, taking notes as if I was learning a new subject in school. This time, the subject was cancer.

I was devastated as the surgeon explained how he would literally play a horrific game of connect the dots on my face. In the end, the final picture would be a horrible reminder of having faced cancer. He would start at the site of the tumor and mark 2 centimeters north, 2 centimeters south, 2 centimeters east, and 2 centimeters west along my face to then connect the points and create a circle. Then just like using an ice cream scooper he would dig deep to rid my face of this disease.

"Next we will determine which lymph nodes may also be carrying cancer. I'll cut out two to three lymph nodes to test them."

Another scar, I thought to myself.

I knew from my own research that once Merkel Cell reaches the lymph nodes, the chances of it metastasizing and ultimately spreading to the liver, lungs, and brain are high. Merkel Cell likes to travel at high speeds and thrives on the opportunity to race to different parts of the body. In cases where it has spread, most patients don't live beyond nine months.

The doctor presented each scenario. "If the margins are clear and your lymph nodes show no signs of cancer, you will have a second surgery to close the hole on your face and your treatments may be over. If the margins are not clear, we will dig again during a second surgery to attempt to clear all of the cancer and you will need radiation. If the cancer has spread to the lymph nodes, you will need both chemotherapy and radiation." But we would have to be patient because the only way to determine which scenario would fit me would be to have the first surgery and wait for the results.

I had questions for sure, but didn't know exactly what to say. Speechless, I sat there as if the information didn't mean anything to me. I was almost ignorant in understanding what was about to happen. And so I waited and I sat still and time passed.

Then I realized I wanted to know how I would look when the surgery was over. I guess I had been so concerned about living, so set on being strong, that I hadn't thought about the long-term ramifications for my face.

Suddenly facing cancer was not just about the treatments, the surgeries, the chance of dying, but it was also about me as a woman. I think it hit me and I knew I would never look the same. So I asked "the question," curious to know my fate.

"How will I look when this is all over?" I spoke softly as the doctor listened.

"You won't look like a monster," he said. Those were his *exact* words!

Really? I thought. *Am I supposed to be happy with that answer? I never even considered that I could look like a monster.*

A monster? What exactly did he mean? Was I supposed to find comfort in knowing that I wouldn't look like a monster?

"Listen, you are a very attractive woman so I want to be honest and tell you that you will never look the same."

Thanks for the compliment, I thought sarcastically. My head was cloudy. I was getting a little pissed off.

"In time you will heal and look just fine," the doctor reassured me.

And with that, we began to make plans to destroy my face.

We were taken to a second office to wait as the nurse scheduled my surgery. Merkel Cell is time-sensitive, grows fast, and spreads rapidly. I was scheduled for surgery quickly, but began to wonder if I should seek a second opinion.

Mark and I were left alone to discuss the information before finalizing the surgery date. It was then that I fell apart. It was the way he looked at me, so lovingly, so deeply in love with me that I knew it would be okay if I cried in front of him.

"My stomach hurts," I told him.

"I know, honey, I know," he said. Mark wrapped his arms around me, held me tightly, and let me cry. Tears streamed down my face. I knew that what really mattered was my ability to beat this cancer, but for a moment, I allowed myself to mourn my face.

As a woman, I felt devastated to think about what I might look like. My whole life I had spent time putting on make-up, taking care of my appearance, and caring about how I looked. I enjoyed taking care of myself. And ironically, my whole life, my favorite physical feature had been my face. Being short, I always felt my legs were a little too chubby. I liked my body well enough, but there were many days when I just felt chunky. I took care of my hair, but it's thin and not my best feature. So whenever I felt heavy or unhappy with another part of my body, I would always look myself at in the mirror, at my face, and think that I was lucky to have nice skin and a pretty face because that's what people saw the most anyway. I am not at all conceited; it's just that I spent years convincing myself that other parts of my body were not so bad because I had a face I was happy with.

When Mark and I were dating we would spend hours doting on each other. He would always tell me how much he loved my face. I felt less insecure about my large thighs when I was naked in front of him because I knew what he was attracted to the most.

So there I was, learning that my face would never be the same and although I wouldn't look like a monster, I certainly would not be *beautiful*. As Mark held me tight I thought to myself *I want to be pretty for him.* I saw him look at me so many times when we were out with our friends. He looked at me in a way that said *I'm proud of my beautiful wife.* Now I would be different. I knew he would still love me. It wasn't that our relationship was based on shallow appearances, but for a brief period of time, I just felt sorry for myself.

I flashed back to the worst moments in our marriage - the times we argued about dishes or became frustrated with each other over something stupid. Alongside those thoughts were feelings of how madly in love with him I am and how I didn't want to let him down. Immediately I knew that we would never again take each other for granted. Moreover, I saw my daughters' little faces; I remembered the sparkle in their eyes - Danielle's smile and Kaitlyn's laugh - and I began to pull myself together.

We talked about seeking a second opinion, but we knew that Hopkins was a well-known hospital and time was of the essence. Several other doctors recommend Hopkins so we felt confident in moving forward. We gathered our composure and scheduled the first surgery.

That was it. That was the information we had; nothing more. We left the hospital and waited for our future to unfold.

As the path to the unknown unfolded in front of me, I decided to surrender control because I had no choice. I asked God to help me accept my cancer. I realized if I didn't accept it, I couldn't remain peaceful while waiting. In the past, I chose a path of darkness and I wasn't willing to do it again.

I experienced God's love for me and the type of unspeakable peace that comes from knowing Him. I wasn't willing to face cancer alone like I had done with the vertigo. This time, I knew better and I turned to God early on. I had to accept what was happening to me.

After falling apart in the office that day, I was glad I allowed myself the time to mourn, but I was finished with feeling sorry for myself and was now ready to fight for my life.

Still today, I believe that if I focus on the unfair circumstances in life, I fail to accept what I can't change and waste time soaking in the pain. When we stop ourselves from the "blame game" and accept what's facing us, then we begin to feel peace. Whether it's fair, unfair, right, or wrong, if you can't accept your circumstances, you'll miss the lessons along the way.

On my toughest days, I challenged myself to make a list of what I could and could not change. I looked at the list of things that were out of my control and decided to surrender them to God. I began to trust Him and realized that when I gave up control, I experienced peace. I never wanted to "miss out" on the lessons, the blessings, or the gifts He had in store for me. I could only fully experience God's presence when I surrendered control and accepted what I had no control over anyway.

Many of us don't want to accept the difficulties of life and it is a lack of acceptance which causes us to be stuck in negative situations. Sometimes it's just easier to blame God or other people than to face it and accept what you're going through. I know this because it is exactly how I handled the pain of vertigo. It wasn't until I accepted my diagnosis, accepted help, accepted God, and surrendered control that I began to grow.

When it was time for me to accept cancer, I did it with grace.

7

COURAGE

Whenever two or three of you come together in my name,
I am there with you.

Matthew 18:20

In order to be courageous, you must first accept the cards you are dealt. After accepting my diagnosis, I wanted to reach out to my family and help them accept it. I remember the difficulty in waiting. I knew I had to help my family deal with the waiting. I couldn't take away their pain, but I could show them how they could ask God for help just as I did.

I had learned to surrender - surrender all of the pain, all of the doubt, all of the worry. I wanted to guide my family towards surrendering too, so that they could trust God to handle what was ahead.

A few long days after I'd been diagnosed with cancer, I could tell that Mark was hurting. He was distracted and sad. He seemed helpless as he tried to support me.

"I know it sounds a little weird," I told him, "but I've read in the Bible that when two or more people gather in prayer to the Lord that their prayers are heard." I went on to explain that I believed in prayer and I hoped that we could pray together.

"I will do anything if you think it will work," he told me. We had never prayed together before and although it was a little awkward at first, we quickly fell deeper in love by drawing closer through our pain.

On the first night, I told him that I wanted to pray with a candle I bought at our church. I purchased it at a fundraiser for a young girl with brain cancer. Although I didn't know her, I found strength in knowing that she too was fighting and that the candle would bring hope to both of us. Little did I know at the time, the same little girl would play a very significant role in my life, much later.

"You pray first," he told me. "I'm not sure what to say."

"Usually I talk to God like I am talking to a friend," I told him since I had no idea how he prayed and I didn't want him to feel uncomfortable.

"Sounds good," he replied nervously.

In the beginning it felt weird to pray with my own husband! During religious discussions in the past, he liked to remind me that he was an "Alter Boy" during his entire childhood – and he never missed a Sunday – so he was *in good* with the *Big Man* upstairs. Spirituality was an area of our marriage I was excited to grow. I had never shared a prayer experience with anyone so intimately.

At first we laughed a lot, sort of nervous laughter I guess, but I knew God enjoyed our sense of humor – we felt His presence even when we cracked a few jokes during our prayers!

The closeness I felt to Mark as we prayed each night was unlike anything I had previously experienced. With him by my side, I was able to release my fears, anger, and sadness, and my hope was restored. We connected in a new way, as if we were falling in love all over again. But falling in love was better this time because we had the comfort of already knowing each other and the life we'd built together.

Within a few nights I began to see a dramatic change in Mark. His new prayer life was truly affecting him and for me this was a beautiful experience. He began to act like himself again. He was relaxed, peaceful, and certainly more hopeful about my diagnosis.

Nothing changed in terms of the information we received. We were still waiting and wondering, but we felt different. Now we were determined to fight this beast together. Peace replaced pain and we were calm once again.

I prayed for that same peace to restore my parents' broken hearts. My mom was familiar with the power of prayer and I knew she would find her own way of dealing with the waiting. But I worried about my father. He had always been an incredible man, a man of strength, a man filled with love for his family, but my dad was hardly a religious man. He's funny and loud, tattooed, and a bit intense. And he worries – a lot. He called me often and probably drove my mom a little crazy. He wanted answers. Helping him remain peaceful was a challenge. I prayed for him and asked God to protect his anxious heart.

Soon after, I was shocked when he shared with me a book that he'd read. Seriously, I have never known my dad to read! He is a very intelligent person, but not someone who reads regularly or *ever* for that matter. I guess in his own way he was searching; searching for answers, for reasons, for relief from his pain.

"You should read this," he recommended. Looking at the title, *When God Lets You Down*, I knew I would find greater strength in reading someone else's story. Excited, I read it right away. It was an incredible story of a young pastor and his wife who watched their baby die in front of them. They experienced many miscarriages to only later feel devastated when they lost their first-born child. They had been faithful people their entire lives, but the pain they experienced caused them to doubt God. The story was raw and real – helpful in so many ways.

I believe my father found comfort in knowing that a pastor could doubt his faith because it made his doubt seem okay. He realized that faith doesn't mean we never question God. He could understand how the pastor felt so let down. The author went on to describe his journey back to God. He was able to restore his belief in God by witnessing the outpouring of love around him. It was the undying love of the people in his life who reminded him that God is full of love and wants only to heal our broken hearts.

My father watched as people poured their love out to me. It's true that we've never seen God, but the people who carry Christ in their hearts represent the type of love God has for each of us. It was the way my family and friends stopped everything to comfort me that truly opened my father's eyes to the power of love and faith.

An amazing friend of mine organized a celebration in honor of me. Everyone celebrated my life by testifying their faith in God to me. They wrote scripture on beautiful note cards, wore pink bracelets that read: "Faith, Survivor, and Hope." They were unselfish, giving, and kind. It was the type of love that signified what faith is really all about – believing in the unseen. I felt their love and their commitment to my survival. It wasn't that they gave me a tangible gift – it was in their touch, in their hearts, and in their faith that I knew I was so deeply loved.

As my most faithful friends and family prayed for me, I could feel what I could not see. When someone is facing devastating circumstances, it is the prayers and outpouring of love that will give that person the courage to fight.

I personally experienced God's presence in the people who love me the most and I'm better equipped today to reciprocate that love to others.

Strangers prayed to God in support of me. People I didn't even know were rooting for me. Why? Why would anyone who didn't even know me care so much about my fight? Obviously people who have faith are able to give love to others the way God expects us to – unselfishly and unconditionally – and I witnessed that goodness in people.

What provokes a person to exude love or hatred? What provokes a person to smile or curse at a stranger? What provokes a person to give or take from another? I believe people who are courageous enough to love God also understand the power of connecting to every other human on this earth.

It's the connection found between people of faith that proves God is full of love for His people. Just by witnessing a person's behavior, it can be obvious how deeply God lives within that person. You can see it in the eyes of strangers – the peace or pain that resides in their soul. When we try, we can see past appearances and into the eyes of a person to witness serenity or a void within their soul. I'm rooting for everyone to feel peace each day by knowing God fully.

A few days later my dad arrived at my house with a new surprise – a tattoo on his wrist that read, "Faith." It was unbelievable to me that he had come so far without having the exact answers he was looking for. His tattoo signified his belief in the *unseen* and his commitment to hope even under the worst circumstances. To me, he was courageous and I loved him more than ever before.

There is no doubt that my strength comes from my relationship with God. I never want to force my beliefs on anyone, but I truly wish that everyone would take a chance and trust God instead of becoming angry, bitter, or resentful when dealing with hardship. I only share my faith because I have felt the power of the unseen living within my heart and the transformation that occurred within my family during this time.

God never sat face to face with me as I prayed, but it certainly felt like it! His comfort washed over me and filled me with peace and strength. I know this closeness prepared me for my future battles. I try not to judge others based on religious beliefs, but at the same time I sincerely wonder what our world would be like if everyone felt the Holy Spirit radiating through the depths of their soul.

I felt the Holy Spirit envelope me as I prepared for my first surgery. I was courageous after I prayed to God and allowed Him to guide me through this uncertain path.

On the morning of my first surgery I was sent for an initial test to reveal which lymph nodes should be removed and tested. Lymph nodes, I learned, are found all over our bodies. They are the "filters or traps" that usually promote proper functioning of the immune system. Lymph nodes with cancer are inflamed or enlarged. For me, it was important to determine the drain pattern, the path that Merkel Cell would follow after spreading from the initial tumor. Since Merkel Cell is not willing to remain still, it was obvious that in time the cancer would spread if not caught early enough. Since the original tumor was found on my face it was likely that the cancer would travel from the original site and land itself inside the lymph nodes found in my neck. Once Merkel Cell arrives in the lymph nodes, it quickly works its way to other parts of the body.

The nurse injected dye into the site of my tumor. Six tiny needles were applied to my cheek. The hot sting of each needle made me flinch. Since childhood, I had been poked with plenty of needles and although I was strong, I found this irritating. But I remained calmed, and concentrated on positive thoughts.

Each needle injected a radioactive die that lit up inside of me giving a 95 percent chance of properly detecting which lymph nodes were likely to be carriers – to determine if the cancer had already spread.

"We found two or three likely carriers," I was told. With a black sharpie, the doctor made circles on my skin. The black circles indicated the lymph nodes underneath that needed to be extracted during surgery. I felt a sigh of relief just knowing I made it through one more painful experience.

I am strong, I reminded myself. *I can handle this because I choose my own attitude and I am in control of my thoughts.*

One last look in the mirror and I knew I was mentally ready for another surgery.

8

MONSTER

Trust in the LORD with all your heart.
Proverbs 3:5 (New International Version)

I am not the monster. Merkel Cell is the monster. I know I'm beautiful because God made me and I am a direct reflection of Him. Facing my new "face" isn't about me - it's about showing the world what power there is in prayer, faith, and love. Because these three flow through me, I will defeat Merkel Cell. This disease has no idea how strong I really am.

March 2007 - First Facial Surgery

The doctor greeted me with a smile on the morning of my surgery. I felt ready, but I had one major concern. In the past, I had become severely ill as a side effect of anesthesia. This time, an incredible concoction of medication was given to me. They called my dose the *full court press* and every measure was taken to improve my chances of not having a negative reaction to the anesthesia. Additionally, the nurses were amazing and kind. Luckily, I woke up from the surgery without a reaction to the anesthesia. And I was thrilled that my hospital stay involved only one night. The next day, I was able to come home and rest.

At home I finally looked at myself for the first time. *Dear Lord, what has happened to me?* I had a bright yellow bandage sewn *into* my face. The bandage covered most of my left cheek and was shaped like a piece of cauliflower! Maybe it was the pain killers or the shock of it all, but I wasn't upset

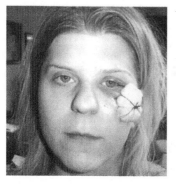

and had yet to cry. For reasons, I can't fully understand, I felt happy. Peace came from knowing that I was fighting this cancer. I knew I was going to win and I was determined to remain peaceful. *This too shall pass and one day, I will look normal again.* For now I would just have to accept where life had me at the moment. I felt God's peace running through every part of my body.

About a week after the first surgery, it was time to return to the doctor's office to uncover what was underneath the flower sewn to my face. I was nervous, of course, but I held a positive attitude. I made a choice to beat this cancer – it wouldn't destroy my soul.

Maybe cancer had damaged my face, maybe the road ahead of me would be long, maybe there would be moments where I'd cry or feel sad, but I was committed to victory. I would not let cancer take over what mattered to me the most – my loving spirit, my soul, or my relationships with the people who loved me.

As the doctor cut off the flower, as we called it, I sat still...ready to win. I looked in the mirror and held my breath.

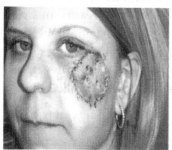

My mom was with me at the time and I'm sure she wanted to cry, but didn't. She was strong.

While looking in the mirror at the doctor's office, I saw a beautiful woman staring back at me. I saw a woman who knew she was loved and would not give up fighting. I really liked who I saw looking back at me – regardless of appearance.

The nurse re-bandaged my face and sent me home to wait. We would have to receive the pathology report in order to know if the margins were entirely clear.

With Merkel Cell the best you can do is clear out as much cancer as can be seen under a microscope. Once the margins are clear, the doctors can stop *digging*. I knew the power of Merkel Cell – that it could linger behind in one tiny cell, unrecognizable through a microscope, but strong enough to grow and form a tumor again. But I was not counting on that! I believed that I would conquer this beast and I never stopped believing in my survival – even when the test results weren't as favorable as I hoped.

Finally, the results revealed that my lymph nodes were clear. Praise God! The margins, however, were not. The cancer was still lingering and I needed additional surgery.

Late-March 2007 – Second Facial Surgery

By this time, the chief of plastic surgery at John's Hopkins was heavily involved in my case. The cancer had spread to my skeletal muscles and it was difficult for doctors to get a clear margin after just one surgery. The surgeon made me feel calm. He was encouraging and his staff was comforting. They took care of me emotionally and ensured me that I would recover!

Most of the second surgery was a blur. It was always the "reveal" that I anticipated the most – the moment where I'd uncover my face, take off the bandages, and view the aftermath. During this surgery doctors removed every part of my left cheek – cutting down into the bone and removing all tissue and fat.

The hole in my face was enormous, deep, and bloody. By now, I was in pain. Most every moment of the day, I covered the damage to allow proper healing. I also wanted to protect my children from seeing their mommy who really did resemble *a monster.*

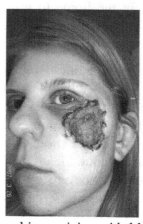

Many times while wearing dressings to cover the wound, I felt something dripping down from the site of destruction. The first time I felt the sensation it was as if something was trickling down my cheek, like water, but different. I went to my bathroom to privately explore the issue. I looked at myself in the mirror and saw blood trickling down my face. A disgusting smell permeated the room. It was as if my flesh was melting, mixing with blood, and dripping out and through the bandages. My flesh, bone, nerves, and tissue had been carved away. Still, the aftermath of the surgery was slowly seeping out making its presence known.

I pretended for a moment that this nightmare was over and instead filled my mind with new images. I created a new scene where I was sipping wine with my girlfriends and we were laughing at the silly things good friends laugh about. I thought of all of the amazing friends in my life; from different circles, but each important...

Childhood friends like Tierney who would encourage me and then help me create the perfect hairstyle to cover the scar; college friends like Ellyn, Elizabeth, Melanie, and Jen Paige who would bring me a few more drinks, keep me laughing and stay up late talking all night long; close friends like Tracey, Missy, Brandi, and Jen who would take me to the spa and help me relax; all of Mark's friends (that had become my friends!) who would take me out to celebrate my recovery; neighbors like Sherry, Dorothy, and Judy who would take the girls out for some fun so I could rest; spiritual friends like Linda, Melissa, and Sally who would talk to me about God's role in all of this...I began to imagine eating crabs with my family, Mark's family, my sisters-in-law, our nieces and nephews, and our parents.

I saw everyone who mattered to me and after awhile, I forgot about the real reason I was staring at myself in the first place.

Mid-April 2007 – Third Facial Surgery

By now, we were told the margins were clear and it was time to put my face back together – hoping for the best possible results. This time the goal was to *close* the hole by placing my skin over top the damaged area. Once again, I was put to sleep. I would wake up to more bandages, more swelling, and a new face – one that displayed the aftermath of cancer in a more permanent way.

A few days later, I sat on the floor of my bathroom with the left side of my face dressed in white bandages; ready to remove the cover to see how the hole in my face had been *closed.*

I sat still ready to uncover the next step. *Meredith, you've done this before.* I laughed and cried at the same time and somehow had the strength to smile. *It can't be any worse than it was before!* Deep down, I knew that this reveal would be more permanent than the others. I looked directly into the mirror, into my own eyes, and felt tranquil. I slowly uncovered the bandages and sat motionless. I was determined to embrace my appearance. And so I did.

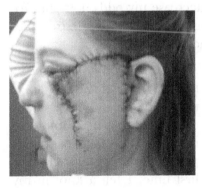

Now I had to face my scar – one that covered most of my left cheek. I realized that with time it might fade, but that it was a scar that I couldn't hide. My face was too swollen to really see the permanent impact the previous surgeries actually had.

I knew it looked worse in that moment than it would in the end and somehow knowing that gave me hope.

As time went by and my face healed, I made peace with my large scar. It was a part of me now – a part I would have to accept.

I began to wear my hair differently; parting it in a way that covered some of the damage. But even the most perfectly placed hair couldn't cover my scar entirely. I had a choice – to crumble and hide or to redefine my own beauty. It was my choice.

Radiation, summer 2007

It took six weeks of daily radiation to make my doctors feel more confident that they had done everything possible to kill this cancer. Merkel Cell can initially respond to chemotherapy, but doesn't always give the long-term advantages that come from radiation. Three out of four doctors we consulted suggested I receive a rather large dose of radiation to provide the best chances of avoiding a reoccurrence.

Merkel Cell reoccurs 50 percent of the time. I had a 1 in 2 chance of facing cancer again, but with radiation, my odds of remaining free of Merkel Cell cancer were much greater. I was told, however, that radiation causes cancer. I knew that being exposed to such a large dose would increase my chances of facing cancer later. I could decrease my odds now and *live* or take the chance of allowing Merkel Cell to destroy me. Prayerfully, I agreed with the radiation protocol.

At first, I found it unsettling to have my head locked to a radiation table. A mask was created to match the mold of my face. As the mask was placed over my face for the first time, I felt a knot in my throat, but only allowed a few tears to slip away.

I had to quickly find a sense of humor. *I could win any Halloween costume contest. Even if I won the pity vote, I'd still win.* Seriously, I looked like Jason from the movie, *Friday the 13*.

Little did I know at the time that Mark would help us all find humor in my mask! Months later at Danielle's Halloween-inspired birthday party, Mark surprised the kids by playing chase in the backyard with my mask on his face. They laughed and screamed, ran and hid, but had the time of their lives. I stood on the deck watching – laughing out loud – remembering the hell we'd been through and then became proud that we could find fun in something so serious.

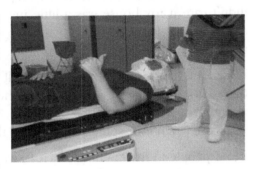

The hard, plastic mask fit my head tightly and exposed radiation only to the affected areas. I would not let this daunt me. I had to be brave.

I laid still and prayed as the radiation entered my body. *Protect me Lord and use the radiation to kill only my bad cells. Restore my health completely so that I can fully live to testify my love for you.*

After about three weeks or so, I faced myself in the mirror, once again, and was humbled. My face was beat red from the radiation but in that perfect moment, I was alive! I developed a new respect for myself – a deeper love for who I was and how I was living.

On the outside, I looked different, but on the inside I was changing and growing and learning to deal with the stress of cancer.

One major stress was learning to deal with episodes of suspicion during follow-up CT scans. At one point, a possible reoccurrence of Merkel Cell was suspected along with the possibility of thyroid cancer! Peace that can only come from knowing God kept me calm as I continued with test after test – waiting for more results.

Today, I remain most grateful for the lessons I learned during these painful times. These lessons are gifts from God and I cherish them. They have changed my soul.

The lessons that mean so much to me are the pieces that make up the top layer of my spiritual cake. I began to enjoy life in a new way! I ate chocolate chip cookies without guilt, didn't care if my house was a little messier than normal, and didn't think twice about staying in my pajamas on the weekend!

I was alive and grateful. I gave myself permission to live – fully. I stopped worrying about all of the tiny things we worry about! I kissed Mark more often and forgave my daughters with ease when they spilled milk on the floor.

I told people in my life how much I loved them and never left anyone without a hug. I was beginning to live the way Jesus intended – with love and peace radiating my soul.

Today, I continue to feel peace because I learned to embrace my spirituality. There are moments in which I become stressed, easily irritated or frustrated with the "normal' aspects of life – motherhood, marriage, responsibilities, but I stop myself now and remember how far I have come and the importance of my spirit. I am and will continue to enjoy the best part of my spiritual cake. My journey is far from over and my story continues on, but I know that even with set-backs, I'm committed to living my very best life.

9

PEACE

I give you peace, the kind of peace that only I can give. It isn't like the peace that this world can give. So don't be worried or afraid.

John 14:27

It is possible to have peace each day. My prayer life has led me to live a life of peace. When my doctor removed a suspicious spot after I was certain my cancer was in remission, it was daily peace, the kind of peace you need every day to tackle life that got me through all the waiting. I was blessed with the news that my cancer had not returned and the spot they excised was nothing - just an innocent growth. Daily peace gave me permission to breathe.

With the prospect of facing thyroid cancer, I remained collected, unruffled, and steady. When you endure so much in such a small amount of time, you are changed forever. I knew I wanted to be proud of how I changed. I knew it was within my control to manage my feelings and redirect my thoughts because this was pleasing in the eyes of God. My test results came back negative for thyroid cancer and I praised God not only for favorable test results, but also for the ability to remain calm during the chaos.

Daily peace is only something that comes with a lot of practice. I remember a time when I neglected to pray for daily peace and something so meaningless became such a frustrating part of my life.

There are little things that can be so annoying about dealing with cancer's aftermath. Obviously, there are serious issues such as financial devastation, family stress, side effects of chemotherapy or radiation, and recovering from surgery. I handled most of the *big* stuff pretty well. In fact, I often surprised myself after each surgery when I had to "face my new face" or deal with the pain.

But there were small complications – little things that would sneak up and frustrate me! As a result of deep digging to my left cheek, I had no padding, cushion, or support on that side. At random times when my daughters and I hugged, our heads would bump and they accidentally came in contact with my face. Each time, the pain was excruciating, to say the least. It took my breath away. My whole world stopped each time it happened. Mark and I talked to them about being very careful around *mommy's face.* They were always careful, but as a mom you are constantly carrying your young children, snuggling, wrestling, and playing which requires contact.

One morning, Danielle was leaving for Kindergarten and she and I reached for each other to hug before she got on the bus. In an instant, it happened. We bumped heads and I immediately felt a pit in my stomach. I can't explain how hard it was for me to catch my breath. I couldn't let her know I was in pain. I sent her off with a smile on the outside, but inside my face stung. It burned with pain.

How can I live like this? I began to wonder. *I can't live like this forever.* Somewhere inside I knew I needed reconstructive surgery, but I wasn't ready for more doctor appointments, hospitals, and the long process necessary to restore my face.

Within minutes, the pain subsided. But, the next morning I woke up with a huge puffy eye on the damaged side of my face.

It didn't hurt anymore, but it was incredibly irritating. For the first two days I was so busy at work and home that I honestly just ignored it. I was tired anyway and thought that it might be a reminder that I needed more rest. By day three, I was frustrated.

Why did I let this bother me so much? Well, I'm human and I become frustrated just like you. Complications from cancer are usually more serious than a puffy eye, but this time I'd had enough! It wasn't the bruise that bothered me. Certainly I'd seen myself look much worse. It wasn't painful anymore. However, I couldn't put my finger on the root of my frustration.

A little puffy eye shouldn't matter, right?

Wrong! Sometimes it does. I never considered praying about my eye or giving any of my smaller burdens to God. But, I should have prayed. I should have given it all to God.

When dealing with all the large-scale effects of our struggles, sometimes we forget the importance of what we consider small things. My faith carried me through everything up to this point, but it seemed silly to rely on faith for this!

Then it hit me. If I could feel so much peace during such dark times, I should rely on that same faith to help me with the small, irritating parts of life. My faith certainly could have made this small stuff easier to deal with.

I realized in that moment that I needed my faith for all my stuff - big, small, annoying, frustrating, joyous, overwhelming, and everything in between. I wish I'd invited Him into my life at the moment Danielle and I bumped heads. I didn't have to deal with that alone. If I prayed to God for comfort, my mood would have been better, calmer, and kinder.

So with time, ice, and a heating pad, my eye healed and it turned out the swelling was nothing more than a reaction to the head bump between Danielle and I as we hugged at the bus stop earlier that week.

Learning about daily peace and how to be peaceful during smaller issues has become a huge blessing. In fact, much of my life today is about the *small* stuff. I no longer face kidney disease, debilitating vertigo (although I do experience mini-episodes), or cancer, so everything else seems pretty small. But I am human and most days, life presents some type of small, irritating issue that can potentially leave me feeling desperate.

Instead, I go back to this lesson – knowing God through daily prayer allows me to feel peace while dealing with all aspects of life.

Daily prayer sets me on the right path and gives me peace. Prayer is like exercise – if you don't do it, the results will fade. Today I spend much of my quiet time in prayer. I pray very informally, talking to God as my best friend. I share my feelings, desires, and needs and I praise Him for all His blessings. It's the daily conversations with God that make my life so complete.

Although daily peace is the most rewarding lesson of all, it's the one I struggle with the most. Life is busy. I am an extremely ambitious and driven person. My mind and body move fast and I sometimes forget to take time for prayer.

A relationship with God is a lot like a microwave! When you put a little time into heating things up, the results are quick and powerful. Prayer is my power. Sometimes I spend a long time in prayer, but most of my daily interactions with God are through quick, powerful prayers that heat me up and make me ready to face the world. Like putting food in a microwave, it only stays hot for so long. I have to exercise my powerful relationship by heating it up often with quick and easy methods when it comes to my prayer life. Not all food can be cooked in the microwave, however, and we all know that the best meals take time. The same is true of prayer. I do crave longer periods of quiet time with God so that I can actually hear what He has to say to me! When I am in need of a quick fix, however, I can turn to God and ask Him for what I need at the moment.

I need these quick prayers – especially when dealing with rude people. Those who are rude, careless, and quick-to-judge do get under my skin! Although, I have to admit that I can be all of these things at times.

I'm often reminded that the way you treat people is reflected back in how others treat you. Generally, I have a lot of cheerful interactions with people and most who know me would probably agree that I'm a positive person. But I'm not perfect and of course I make mistakes. I've been rude to the cashier at the grocery store when I'm in a hurry and he's moving too slow! I can be so wrapped up in what I want to say that I forget to listen to the other person. Sometimes after a long day at work, I'm grumpy toward my husband who hasn't even done anything wrong!

We all fail to keep and spread our peace at certain times. I realize that ill behavior toward me is only a reminder of how I want to live - a life of forgiveness, love, and peace. I have learned not to let the hurtful behavior of others rob me of my peace, but I have also become truthful about my behavior and have to admit when I'm wrong.

When my relationships or interactions feel strained, I look back at myself through my own social mirror. *How have I treated others around me? Am I saying or doing things out of pride? How much time have I prayed and asked God to shape me?*

I invite you to think about your behavior toward strangers, your family, friends, and co-workers, before judging their behavior toward you. Sometimes people are just simply unhappy. I say *love them and leave them.* Do not fall victim to their behavior - instead, remain positive and move on. And say a sincere prayer for them!

Taking personal responsibility for your own behavior through daily prayer will help you remain positive in your interactions with people in a way that will not tamper your soul. Just ask God to show you how.

I *need* daily peace. It's in my control and yours, too! Sometimes I find joy in buying a new outfit or eating a warm bagel. Happiness temporarily comes from taking the day off or planning a fun vacation. But this is different. Peace *never* leaves. God gives peace in a way that cannot be replaced or compared to our possessions, accomplishments, or talents. Peace that comes from knowing God surpasses all other joy. It's unshakable and nothing can destroy it.

10

HUMILITY

*You, LORD, are our Father. We are nothing but clay, but
you are the potter who molded us.*

Isaiah 64:8

Over time life became more normal and I was able to step
back and reflect on all I had been through. Still needing
reconstructive surgery, but not ready to begin the process, I
was ready to move forward and live life fully. At this point, I
had a lot of growing to do and there were many life lessons
just waiting for my discovery! I sincerely hope I never stop
growing...I hope that's your desire, too.

By now I was ready to fully enjoy the top layer of my spiritual
cake! If you recall, this is the layer where I truly began
savoring life by growing deeper into the person God created
me to be. It all started with a willingness to dig deep inside of
myself.

My cancer therapy didn't involve just radiation. Regaining
normalcy in my life also helped tremendously. Part of this
involved shopping for meals, making sure we had enough
diapers on hand, and taking care of the daily tasks we are all
responsible for! I remember leisurely strolling through the
aisles of one of my favorite stores enjoying my popcorn and
diet soda. I felt happy, relaxed, and just about ready to leave
(with several items that were not on my list)!

"Excuse me, excuse me," I heard from a distant voice in the
background. I turned around to see a somewhat familiar face.

"I don't know if you remember me, but you taught one of my graduate courses a few semesters ago," the young teacher went on to explain how we knew each other.

"Yes, I do remember you," I said. She had a new baby with her.

With a big smile on my face I braced myself as she asked, "How are you?"

It was the type of question that indicated *I know something was previously wrong with you so I am asking because the last time I saw you, you were not well.*

I was confused for a moment. Thoughts ran rapidly through my mind. *Did I teach her the semester I was diagnosed with cancer and had to stop teaching in the middle of the semester? Or was she referring to the terrible vertigo that plagued my life for so long?*

"I'm great!" I responded with an over-the-top amount of enthusiasm. I remembered quickly that I hadn't seen her in a long time.

"Your baby is adorable," I went on to make conversation.

"Thank you!" she smiled.

Of course in the back of my mind, I'm thinking of the huge scar on my face. It wasn't even just the scar, but it was the way my face was now indented – carved out on the left side. It's not that I was embarrassed by my appearance; it was that my appearance made a statement. It left unanswered questions for her, I knew.

Feeling like I owed her an explanation, I said "I don't know if you heard, but I was diagnosed with cancer in February."

"Oh I'm so sorry." She looked sad. In her eyes I could see her sincerity. She must have felt sorry for me after witnessing my vertigo the semester I taught her and now she knew that I'd faced cancer.

"It's okay really, I feel great and I am doing well." I smiled. "The cancer was on my face (fulfilling my need to explain the scar), but I'm healthy and finished with my treatments."

She said all of the right things and we quickly ended the conversation.

On that day, at that moment, I felt embarrassed, again, for who I was and for what I had endured.

It was all I could do to make it to my car before I began to cry.

What a ridiculous story I have.

I felt self-conscious and judged. She didn't say or do anything to affirm my negative feelings. It was me! I just hated my story for the moment.

How are you should just be one of those polite questions to which *fine* is appropriate and that should be the end of it. I remembered that the summer I taught her was when my vertigo was at its worst. I wasn't driving at that time and during one class, I had to dismiss early due to an attack. My entire class saw me at a very vulnerable time in my life.

Standing in that store, I just wanted to say *I'm fine* and leave it at that. But I felt I owed her something more. If I were her, I would honestly wonder what happened and why there was such a large, new scar.

Just like I questioned myself as a small child, I began to wonder if all of this was my fault. *Aren't I past this stage yet?* Although I'm not perfect, I've always taken care of my body, lived a life of as little stress as possible, and spent plenty of time laughing. Rationally, I knew that the last few years of illness were not my fault, but I was afraid of being judged.

My peace was stolen because I allowed it to be. I worried what someone else thought of me more than I worried about what I thought of myself!

I had a chance now to learn a new lesson from God.

I needed God to finish breaking me - to shape me as a potter shapes his clay. I prayed that God would take away negative feelings that were buried deep within my soul. God allowed so much to happen in my life and ultimately broke me so that He could reshape and reform me to be better.

I have an invaluable amount of respect and fear for God - He took His time to bless me, break me, teach me, and shape me. He is my father; a parent who loves me more than I can understand. I needed to be broken, once again.

In prayer, I learned how to be humble. I learned to stop worrying so much about what other people thought. I wanted to fully experience God's presence and peace in my life, once more. In order to do that, I had to be more humble and less prideful.

In order to savor life I had to be willing to become who God created me to be.

The opposite of humility is pride. I'm not talking about taking pride in something or when you're proud of someone you love. I'm talking about pride as it relates to arrogance - the kind of pride that pressures you to keep up with another person or provokes you to show off.

I realized that I'd let pride stand in my way of receiving God's peace in this situation, and instead I allowed myself to feel judged. I wanted to study this part of myself; to learn more about my feelings and create a life without prideful thinking. It was pride that made me feel embarrassed in front of other people when sharing my story.

So I began reading more books from Christian authors on the subject of pride - I needed and wanted to become more humble. I explored what the Bible taught about pride. I was seeking a soul that worried less about how people judged me, but instead cared more about how I could uplift others. I wanted to stop trying to keep up with everyone else when it came to material possessions or accomplishments. I was seeking a more fulfilling, less prideful, and more humble mentality. With God's love and support, through prayer, I grew tremendously. And I'm still growing!

In my journal I recently wrote: *I surrender my selfish pride to God. My success is not a result of personal advancement, recognition, or salary, but merely a reflection of what the Holy Spirit has called me to do in order to fulfill God's purpose for me.*

The type of freedom I have from knowing Christ is so incredible that I'm compelled to share my most private thoughts. As you read this you may disagree, but I can't hold back how I feel. I only share my deepest thoughts because my experience and beliefs may affect someone, even one person, who is reading my story!

So here goes...

Jesus is the only perfect human being to have ever walked on earth. I realize that I'm not called to be perfect, but today I'm able to receive the Holy Spirit because I've accepted Jesus into my heart. When you receive God's love for you by way of His son Jesus, you can embrace the Holy Spirit and hear God speak to you. God sent his only son, Jesus, to live and die on this earth. Jesus bore all of our sins on the cross - the sins of ALL mankind past, present, and future. Because Jesus took on all of our sins, we can now have a *right* relationship with God. Jesus is the bridge that links us together with God! God has given us a gift - and it's free! It's an amazing, perfect, gift because God loves us so much. "God loved the people of this world so much that he gave his only Son, so that everyone who has faith in him will have eternal life and never really die." - John 3:16

If you've never had a close connection with God, or cannot make sense of how to *listen* to God speaking to you, then you may be missing out on the benefits of the Holy Spirit. You can start today by asking Jesus to become your personal savior. By believing that He performed miracles, demonstrated love, and was an example to guide people towards eternity, you will get to know who He really is.

Not everyone believed in Jesus and many even made fun of Him – but Jesus never became prideful. He never felt the need to do what would make Him popular. He had a purpose and that was to represent His Father's love toward His people. He didn't let pride stand in His way. He suffered, died a horrible death, and was buried in a dark tomb. He rose again, just as God said He would, and then gained the support of His followers because they witnessed the truth being revealed. Can you imagine what the disciples felt when they saw Jesus with their own eyes after they'd just seen him tortured, murdered, and buried?

Today, we do not have the opportunity to see Jesus ourselves. But with the power of the Holy Spirit we can feel His love, presence, and peace. By way of Jesus, God promises to forgive our sins when we seek forgiveness in prayer. Today the Holy Spirit lives in me and *speaks* to me in a quiet whisper that teaches me and guides me from falling victim to pride. Isn't that incredible?

I was broken in a way that I can't fully explain or even understand. However, I'm confident that my suffering has been worth the lessons along the way. Today, I feel greater peace from being completely broken and reshaped into who I was meant to be. By knowing God I learned how to pick up my broken pieces and move on.

By moving closer to the person God intended me to be, I am now able to live a full life – satisfied every day!

11

TRUTHFULNESS

*Keep your lives free from the love of money and be content
with what you have, because God has said, "Never will I leave
you; never will I forsake you."*
Hebrews 13:5 (Today's New International Version)

My life today is different as a result of living with a more
humble spirit. But, I'm no different than any other person
who struggles with temptation and financial stress.

Several years ago, I bought a beautiful, luxurious Lexus SUV.
I loved that car! I mean, I *really* loved that car. Heated seats
and gorgeous leather interior! I felt powerful when I drove my
Lexus.

I was never boastful about the car, but somewhere deep in my
soul I bought it because I cared about what other people
thought of me. At the time, I was still running a small business
and I needed the car to be a reflection of my success. I never
told anyone that I felt this way and I probably didn't even
recognize these feelings within myself.

One Sunday, Mark and I sat in church with the girls while
listening to our favorite priest, Father Kennedy, deliver
another powerful sermon. On that day, he was talking about
show-offs. He shared a story about two families he knew at a
Catholic school where he was once the lead pastor.

The first family, by all appearances had it all. The parents
were always dressed to the nines. One drove a new Mercedes
and the other a new BMW. Of course, they both had high-
paying jobs. The second family, full of smiles, arrived to

school each day in a clunky car that looked like it might fall apart at any moment. Each morning as they dropped their children off at school, they were kind and friendly...peaceful and positive.

To make his point, our priest shared how he struggled to collect timely tuition payments from the family who appeared to have the most fruitful financial situation. He described the first family as difficult, noting that he often reminded them to pay their bill. The second family had never been late on a tuition payment. Using the behavior demonstrated by the wealthy family, the priest made his point about people who *need* to look good, but have no regard for doing what's right.

He asked us to reflect about showing off in our own lives. He wanted us to think about what we might be doing or not doing to satisfy social appearances. He questioned each of us – making it impossible to deny our own times of showing off.

On the ride home that day, I said to Mark, "You never show off." He has such a quality of humility – I've really never witnessed that type of behavior in him. I praised him for his mild-mannered, humble attitude. In praising Mark, I was forced to look at my own behavior. Thoughts came flooding into my head. *Okay, there was that time and maybe one other – well, that doesn't make me a show-off does it?* Isn't it funny how we justify or talk ourselves out of something? At that moment, God was convicting me of this behavior.

It wasn't that I considered myself rude or cocky. In fact, I'd always been a very friendly person. It wasn't that I showed off to make others look bad and I certainly didn't show off in every aspect of my life. But somehow in my late 20s and early 30s, I felt a need to keep up with everyone else when it came to money. I never wanted to appear as if I didn't have enough. After all I'd been through I had developed a weird sense of entitlement about money. I thought I deserved to overlook the truth about my finances and spend more than I really had.

After battling cancer, my small business had truly crumbled. I was making less money than ever before and I felt differently about the direction of my career path. I decided to return to my original passion, teaching, and close my business. I was really trying to dig deeper into my own self during this time. I was waiting on God to guide me and show me more about His plan for my life. The same thought kept repeating over and over in my mind - it was time to become truthful about my finances.

It's interesting how the Holy Spirit can speak to us if we're willing to listen. Sometimes, it takes the form of repetitive thoughts. Or, out of nowhere, God can drop a thought or idea into your spirit that helps you make a decision. God speaks through people around you, through things you hear, and material you read. The key is listening and trying to decipher God's direction versus your own thoughts about what's best for you.

So when I felt God was encouraging me to recognize that our finances needed attention, I humbly accepted the challenge. Mark has always been very conservative - a saver and planner - but we both threw a lot of our plan out the window simply because life had been crazy. We did what we could to make ends meet. Luckily we (really, Mark) had a bit of savings to help us when my business was failing or when I worked less during each health struggle. But now it was time to be honest about our financial situation.

After dealing with such terrible vertigo and beating cancer, I learned a lot about being humble. But facing the truth about our finances was one of the most humbling experiences of all! Can you relate?

It was obvious that I needed to work more hours in a secure field, like teaching. I also needed to continue supplementing my income by teaching graduate level classes to other teachers. And the most important goal was to spend less.

The first step was learning to let go of my Lexus. I found myself, soon after, waking up every morning and going to work driving a low-end Honda Civic with no power windows, no power locks, and no heated seats.

I felt liberated! I am humble when I drive that car. It is reliable and costs virtually nothing to drive. Honestly my car today is the worst car I've ever driven by all material standards. Even as a teenager, I had a car with power locks and power windows! However, my car reflected the truth about my finances. Now, we're growing our daughters' college funds again, planning and saving for retirement, maintaining our beautiful home, and living with the truth - I don't make enough money to drive a Lexus!

Now don't get me wrong. I like nice cars, beautiful clothes, and fabulous vacations. I don't believe that being humble means you have to give up material pleasures in life. We just have to be careful that we don't define ourselves by material possessions. For me, I'm just being honest and admitting that I'm no longer in competition with anyone and I no longer feel the need to look like I have more money than I actually do.

As Mark and I save more we look forward to trading in my Honda for something nicer one day. I do miss my heated seats, but for now, I have peace knowing that I'm cleaning up my mistakes, making up for lost time (even though my lost time was a result of being ill), and taking responsibility for my careless decisions. I just can't even express how peaceful it makes me feel to have grown into humility. For the first 10 years of our relationship, Mark always drove the cheaper car. He obviously learned about being humble long before me! Today, it is my pleasure that he drives the nicer car although he keeps telling me that he's willing to let me have it. It's not about any car for me; it's about being honest. I feel so good knowing that I don't need a material object to fulfill me.

At the same time, when the time is right, I plan on buying myself something nicer because I'll enjoy the benefits of a more comfortable car, not because I have to keep up with everyone else.

This is an example of what I mean by embracing your top layer of spirituality- savoring life. When you release the ugly, prideful behavior that we've all experienced, at some point, you're truly able to love people instead of trying to keep up with or impress them!

If you're unwilling to recognize pride within yourself, you'll miss out on the sweetest parts of life. We all suffer from it – some more than others – but a full life is one in which you stop doing things because of shallow comparisons and instead do things out of love.

The material possession I am most proud of is our home. It's perfect for our family and I am grateful for every square inch, but want nothing more. Now instead of walking into someone else's house and secretly comparing their home to mine, I feel happy that other people can enjoy nice things. I truly hope that everyone feels peace at home.

Home is the most secure place on earth for me. My hobby is decorating – I'd love to put hardwood floors in our home someday. But now, instead of being bitter or jealous within my soul (remember I would never admit to these things out loud) when I see beautiful hardwood floors in someone's home, I'm truly happy for them and hope they appreciate their floors as much as I know I will someday!

I ask God to keep me humble by praying about this often. It's unnatural and sometimes difficult for me, but the benefits far outweigh the time I take out of my busy schedule to pray each day.

I found it humbling to receive so much support when I faced cancer. My family and friends sent cards, flowers, and home-cooked meals. I felt so loved and that love helped me fight. Daily, people called to ask how I was doing, to tell me they were praying for me, and to offer encouragement. Former co-workers provided meals for an entire week. I hadn't seen any of them in years and there they were ready to support our family. My parents literally dropped everything to come live with our family (again!) so that my daughters would be distracted by ice cream and the fun that comes with having grandparents around! My husband's family reached out with kind words, love, and pure support.

People need to unite during difficult times and unity was one of the most beautiful parts of dealing with cancer.

Seeing people unite to help me and my family was an experience I was so honored to have had. I decided that I had to pay that forward. I knew then that my cancer would have some greater purpose. Having battled cancer would mean that I'd have the opportunity to do something unique with my life – something involving unity. I never wanted to stop witnessing that unity among my family and friends. Clearly, I was ready to guide that unity towards helping someone else because I had been helped so much.

But it was not yet clear to me what God would call me to do. It would take several months, a prayerful journey, and a lot of faith to witness God's plan. I trusted Him. I continued to work on being humble enough to see what He needed me to see. I spent less time thinking about myself and more time thinking about others. I knew the vision would come, but I'd just have to wait. Wait quietly and peacefully.

12

SELF-IMAGE

But the LORD said to Samuel, "Do not consider his appearance or his height, for I have rejected him. The LORD does not look at the things man looks at. Man looks at the outward appearance, but the LORD looks at the heart."

Samuel 16:7 (Today's New International Version)

You've probably heard this before – you were created in God's image. If that's true, then why are we so hard on ourselves?

It's funny how your self- image changes after facing cancer. I must admit, I'm still learning to fully embrace who I am, but I'm certain that facing cancer has brought me closer to my soul in a way that is difficult to explain.

Just like most women, I can be very hard on myself – at times. I'm the first to recognize when I gain extra weight, when my hair needs to be cut, or when my nails look like they've been chewed on by a dog! I'm also the first to notice when I've failed to keep my house clean or be the type of patient mother I need to be.

The image I had about myself *before* cancer was shaped mostly during my childhood and teenage years. I also believe that the image I have of myself *today* was shaped mostly after having faced cancer.

I grew up attending dance classes four or five times each week. My mom owned three dance studios and was a dancer her entire life. For me, I enjoyed the friendships and camaraderie that came with being so involved. Plus, I was the owner's daughter and that made things even better. I knew everyone, felt accepted at the studios, and had many friends.

My experience with dance shaped a lot of what I grew up believing about my body and what I thought it *should* look like. I'm not very tall and, unfortunately, I didn't inherit my mother's long legs. I was never overweight as a young girl, but I certainly wasn't very thin either.

I remember each year our measurements were taken in preparation for our dance recital. Like most young girls, I loved the costumes and performing on stage was awesome, but as I grew older I grew competitive about my measurements. Since my mom owned the studio, I had access to all her files. I would sneak peeks at the measurement charts that she used as a reference when ordering costumes.

As I looked up and down the chart where measurements were recorded, I would compare myself to the other girls on our dance team. Most of the time, my waist was the same or even smaller than the size of the others. Almost always, however, my legs were the largest. I already knew by looking in the mirror and comparing myself during dance class each week that my legs were heavy. Now I had the numbers to prove it.

Looking back, I think I should have tried soccer or softball – an activity that would allow my *muscular* legs to fit in! Spandex, tutus, and fishnet tights...goodness gracious!

The older I got, the chunkier I felt. Looking back, I was not heavy at all, but somehow I chose to compare my worst physical features to the best features of others. By the time I was in college, I knew in my mind that I needed to lose some weight in order feel better when comparing myself to my friends.

On the flip side, I was always pretty likable. I'm in no way sharing my past to sound boastful, but in understanding my own self image, I had to dig deep into my past. In high school, I was our class president for four years, voted "Most Popular" and "Best All-Around." These titles made me feel good and definitely shaped my self- image.

So on one hand, I knew I was well accepted, but by my own bizarre standards, I still wasn't complete. I needed to be thinner in order to fix the voice in my head which reminded me that I would be much more desirable as a size four. I worked for years to get it all right. My weight fluctuated and when I was at my thinnest, I felt most worthy.

This need to be *the best* in all areas of my life made it difficult when I became a mother. Early on, I expected myself to be the best mother to my daughters, at all times. I have a master's degree in education and by all means I know a lot about children. I thought motherhood would be easy for me.

I placed an extreme amount of pressure on myself to get it all right – to provide nutritious meals, implement perfect sleep schedules, and use a loving discipline approach, all while keeping a clean house and trying to be "sexy" for at least thirty minutes once a week! And this went on and on. I failed many times while trying to be the perfect wife and mother.

By the time my daughters were 1 and 3 years old, I realized I was in over my head. Obviously my health issues played a large role in how overwhelmed I felt about motherhood, but the truth is that with or without health struggles, I was completely unprepared for how difficult motherhood would be and how it would change my self-image for the worse.

I realized that "Miss Popular" still had a lot of growing to do. Suddenly there were no titles, no positive recognition, and no reinforcement of who I was by the outside world. Now, I was ordinary – married with children. Many days I was confused about whether I wanted to be a stay-at-home mom or a career woman. I was concerned about what other people thought about my skills as a parent and how my children were behaving. Sometimes I needed a title to confirm who I'd become, but the superlatives were never given out. Have you ever felt this way? It made me feel worthless at times – where were the labels of success from others?

I found myself fighting two terrible illnesses while raising very small children. I had a supportive and loving husband, but some days that just wasn't enough. It wasn't about him; my issues and insecurities were about me.

While I was learning more about God's love for me and was beginning to see my life through His eyes, I still placed a lot of blame on myself when I wasn't perfect. I needed God to help me in a new way. Just as He had broken me in other aspects of my life, I knew it was possible to reshape my thinking about my own self-image. But, I'd not been fully broken and I was in need of a resurrection.

Over time, I learned that just as with everything else in my life, I needed prayer in order to be a better mother and to forgive myself for the times when I made mistakes. Slowly, I started to let go of my need to be *the best* and learned how to be okay with being me – an imperfect human.

I wanted to learn how to love myself fully without needing approval from anyone, but God.

Before cancer, for years, I compared my body to the women around me. Obviously, all of that comparing left me feeling less beautiful than I really was. After facing cancer, I made a conscious decision to be kinder to myself. I knew I deserved to love myself the way God loves me. Once again it was up to me to reach out and ask God to show me how to be kinder to myself when it came to motherhood, my accomplishments, and my body.

I spent time reading books, again, to learn more about how to reshape my thinking and grow into the woman God created me to be. I realized God brought me so far and through so much, that it was pretty shallow to be so concerned about my short legs!

I shared my heart with a girlfriend who could also understand what I was going through. We had similar stories and could relate to each other. We were both ready to make a change; to flip a switch in our minds and be kinder to ourselves.

We decided that the negative voice in our minds created nothing, but lies! My friend had a creative idea – to name that negative voice, as if to separate the lies from the truth. We both agreed that we would name both our voice of truth and our voice of negativity. By naming each, we could identify the truth from the lies. And besides, it was a humorous way to deal with a painful, sometimes debilitating, feeling.

We named the negative voice within us, *Gretchen* (I apologize to any reader who is offended by our name selections) and the positive voice within us, *Mary*.

After many long conversations we were convinced that separating the truth from the lies really made sense! We realized how mean we'd been to ourselves and how peaceful we'd become while rebirthing our positive self-image. So naturally, we wanted to share our thoughts with our other girlfriends!

The following is an expert from an email I wrote to our dear friends:

I'd like to introduce you to Gretchen. She is the voice living inside of you who says things to you that are mean, untrue, and are very negative or disruptive. She prevents you from being who you were really created to be. Mary, however, is the voice of truth. She is the voice that reflects God's love for each of us.

I believe that God created each of us to serve Him and others. The best way I've figured out how to do that is by loving me...all of me.

By loving ourselves, we're able to fill our souls with purity, goodness, grace, mercy, and kindness. This allows us to give back to the world. If we don't love ourselves the way Jesus taught us, then we are offending God. Since God created us in His image and gave us His only son to show His love for us, we respect Him by giving that love back. So, we must love ourselves enough to be able to give to others and share our lives fully.

Mary and Gretchen tend to fight the most in social situations. We all know how hard it can be to prepare ourselves as we face this shallow world. Gretchen has the potential to take over Mary's goodness and compare herself to other women at any given moment. Mary wonders how people perceive her physically because she wants to be accepted in this shallow world. Gretchen loves the opportunity to appear and will often choose a beautiful woman to compare herself to. Mary knows that deep, deep down appearances do not really matter anyway because God thinks she's beautiful, but Gretchen has a way of comparing Mary to others. Poor Mary...isn't this unfair?

Mary is such a good girl, yet Gretchen wants to remind her that she isn't as attractive as the 5' 9', slender, top-heavy, dark-haired woman that is seen only from a distance. Gretchen just can't hide sometimes.

So Mary takes the time to converse with herself. She remembers how sweet she really is and how much she wants to give back to the world. When Gretchen tries to distract Mary from the positive conversation, Mary remembers that she is beautiful because she is humble, kind, caring, and compassionate.

Now don't misinterpret Mary – she enjoys tight jeans, fantastic shoes, and a fresh hairstyle, but not because she needs to fill a void. Mary is proud of her appearance and remembers to embrace who she really is by not comparing herself to others.

Gretchen also shows herself when the house is messy and she reminds Mary that she has neglected to keep a perfect home. She pressures Mary to be a perfectionist. This type of unloving behavior spills over into motherhood and virtually every aspect of Mary's life. Mary must constantly put Gretchen in her place by loving herself more while paying no attention to Gretchen. Prayer works every time and seems to be the most effective way for Mary to conquer Gretchen.

I hope that by sharing Mary vs. Gretchen, you're able to relate to the truth and lies we hear and embrace only the positive messages that you deserve. May God bless you on your journey to identifying your own positive and negative voices so that you can listen only to the truth and never pay attention to the lies. Also know that Mary loves you very much and believes in you more than you realize.

And with that, our circle of friends stopped believing in lies, but began believing in each other.

I've learned to apply the same concept – focusing on the positive and rejecting the negative – to motherhood. I absolutely love being a mom today. I enjoy my daughters so much more now that I'm able to fully embrace motherhood. I no longer worry about silly things. I know that I'm a good mother, that I have the best intentions in mind, and that I don't need an award to confirm my abilities as a mom!

Instead of comparing my skills as a mom to other moms or feeling guilty because I *enjoy* working outside of the home, I simply just enjoy. My daughters are amazing and I wouldn't ever want to miss out on just how great they are!

Raising daughters is fantastic. I think about them as they build their own self-image and I hope that I can be a teacher to them – a teacher that models healthy behavior. I'm committed to only speaking positively about myself in front of them. They will never hear me say that I think I am fat or that I'm not good enough at something. I believe in being honest with them about when I am successful or admitting when I'm not especially talented in a certain area. They know for sure that I am not the best cook, but that I do try!

I want them to know that I can recognize the strengths and needs within myself without modeling self-deprecating behavior. I want them to know that it's important to recognize their talents, admit when they're good at something, but that they don't have to be perfectionists at the expense of living well emotionally.

I often wonder how my journey will impact my daughters. I imagine they may not remember all of the details and for that

I'm glad. But I do hope that my experience will positively impact them - that it will build resilience within them to live life fully and embrace their spirituality!

The gift of a positive self-image has meant a lot to me. More than anything, I want to pass my spirit to my daughters. I love to work hard and I have a lot of dreams to fulfill, but above all my children come first. My biggest dream of all is to raise daughters who have a positive self-image.

Some days I feel blessed by enduring so many changes to my face. I realize that after facing cancer I'm so blessed to be healthy today and I just want to soak up what matters to me the most - the love that I feel from my husband, children, family, friends, and most especially, God. Without God, I would never have the wisdom to change my self-image and love the person God created me to be.

I feel most blessed when I look at myself in the mirror and smile at the 12 scars all over my body; knowing that I'm proud of my life, my story, and me.

Above all, life has become so much sweeter. I love living in the moment, savoring life for all that it is, and embracing the gift of a positive self-image.

And when I fail, because I still do, I become too hard on myself, and let comparisons rob me of my peace. Then, I turn to God - quickly - because in prayer He is the only *sure thing*...and my protection from the shallow world we live in.

13

PURPOSE

*You cannot fool God, so don't make a fool of yourself! You
will harvest what you plant. If you follow selfish desires, you
will harvest destruction, but if you follow the spirit you will
harvest eternal life. Don't get tired of helping others. You will
be rewarded when the time is right, if you don't give up. We
should help people whenever we can, especially if they are
followers of the Lord.*

Galatians 6: 7-10

My purpose on this earth is to serve God by loving people.
That's it. Okay, I realize that it may not be as simple as it
sounds! Loving people is not always easy! But, I believe that in
order to savor life - to live fully - that loving people is
important.

I believe in taking the time to see the best in people and I
hope people will see the best in me. I believe that there is
good inside of *most* people. However, there are people who
are just mean or self-centered and I can't say that I've figured
out how to deal effectively with the dishonest or selfish people
in this world!

I am very far from being perfect. But as I plan my day, map
out the week, and look forward to the months that lie ahead, I
try to keep others first. I fail at times. But mostly I want to
serve God by loving people.

My family will always come first in my quest to fulfill my
purpose. I make mistakes because I will never be perfect, but
my family means everything to me. Putting my husband first

means making sure he has a meal he enjoys because he loves to eat! I love spending time alone with him or going on a date. Our connection grows deeper when together we show kindness to others, listen fully, or laugh out loud at a shared experience. My children also fulfill my purpose in many ways. When I feel impatient, I am reminded to slow down, listen, and take care of them. I let them down sometimes, but my purpose remains the same! I am here to love God first and foremost. Mark and my children come second and fulfill me far greater than I could ever imagine – I know they are gifts from God. And when I take care of them and love them unconditionally, I'm also showing God how much I love Him!

I don't believe that anyone can fully embrace the sweet, savoring parts of life without learning to give joyfully. Without a purpose – one in which your life positively affects others – there will always be a void, a longing for more, a dissatisfaction. When you begin to think more about others and less about yourself, then you are truly living. I want to serve God by giving my best to others.

After a period of searching, deeply, about how I could fulfill my purpose, God spoke to me. This time I was surprised by what He was calling me to do. What I realize today about God is that His greatest rewards, blessings, and plans can only unravel when you are *ready.* Finally, after being broken, shaped, and recreated, I was ready to work for God.

And boy did God have a job offer for me! I remember it clearly – you don't easily forget the times God speaks to you. It was an early morning wake-up call. One that would alter every part of my life!

It was early on a November morning in Ocean City, Maryland when I woke from a deep sleep to hear God's message. Many people don't understand what it means to hear a call from God. Some people are not *quiet* enough to hear what God has to say.

Often I would pray and do all of the talking. *God I need this – God help me with that – God thank you for this.* Over time I learned to be quiet. This time I was actually asleep so it was a good time for God to catch me being still!

I craved God. I wanted to know Him even deeper and learn more about His presence in my life. God, after all, had carried me out of the darkness when I needed Him. This time I wanted to testify, be witness to, share, and tell the world about God in a way that would let people know how much He craved to be close to them.

What would I do with what had happened to me? I needed to feel as if all of my suffering made sense to the glory of God. I had not died. After all, I was healthy again. God deserved the glory.

I am not *always* completely *comfortable* sharing my faith, publicly. In fact, writing so intimately and sharing my faith transparently is a new practice for me. So obviously, not being comfortable preaching on the streets, I wanted to find another way to spread a message – a message of hope. And that's exactly what God decided I should do.

At 4:45 a.m. on that cold November morning I woke up to a message, clearly a message from God that I was to start my own nonprofit organization which would raise money to help cancer patients.

Here I was continuing follow-up treatments from my own battle with cancer, not fully healed, and in need of reconstructive surgery. But somehow I couldn't ignore this message. It had been less than a year since I began my battle with cancer. This seemed crazy.

Have you ever resisted listening to your own parents by thinking that you know better? Has stubbornness ever left you unable to listen to your spouse, sibling, or best friend when they give you much needed advice? Have you ever resisted messages that come from your doctor about eating healthier or exercising more regularly? We all ignore messages or choose not to believe what we know is true sometimes. We also ignore messages from God.

It was only by truly loving God and living each day with Him, as my best friend, that I was able to trust His messages. I didn't really like what God was telling me to do. Start a nonprofit organization? Me? I had a million reasons why this just would not work! And I made a list that went something like this...

1. I have no idea how to run a nonprofit. How would I start? When would I have the time to even think about starting something new?
2. How would this affect Mark and my girls?
3. I don't really want to spend time doing one more new thing. I have so much on my plate right now. I already have goals that I want to accomplish.
4. I might look like a failure. What if this doesn't work out? What if the organization isn't successful and I look like a fool?
5. Why would I want to do something like this right now? Shouldn't I take more time to heal and help myself before helping others?
6. What if there are already organizations out there like this one? Why would I be helpful when larger organization could help people more effectively?

And so on! I wanted to be sure that this was *God* speaking to me. I can only share my own experience, but not seeing God and not being able to have face-to-face conversations with Him meant that on more than one occasion, I misinterpreted my own thoughts as God's will.

In the past, I felt God calling me to do something and then later realized that it was probably just something I came up with myself - this gets easier as your relationship with God grows! The key to understanding God is found within the relationship you have with Him. Remember that by now, I had come to truly know God as my friend. I had opened myself to Him when I had nowhere else to turn. He brought me from pain to peace.

Sometimes your thoughts, personal ideas, or beliefs can be disguised as things we are *called to do*. So how do you know the difference? For me, it comes down to peace. Just as quickly as I thought about saying, "No!" to God regarding His nonprofit idea, a peace immediately washed all my fears away. This peace penetrated my soul and eased my worry. Beyond peace, it's a feeling of comfort knowing that if this is a call from God, all things will work out. God does not call the qualified, but rather qualifies those He calls – those who trust Him. Jeremiah 17:7 reminds us, "But blessed is the man who trusts in the LORD, whose confidence is in him." I knew God would answer my growing list of questions and all my fear would be replaced with a God-given confidence!

Accepting a challenge in today's world usually involves competition – trying to outshine someone else, winning at someone else's expense, or making someone else feel small so you can feel big. To me, accepting a challenge from God is about creating unity among people, testifying to the unconditional love that comes from knowing God, and finding satisfaction in thinking more about others than my own selfish wants. It's about being peaceful with your purpose and being ready; knowing that death is never far and that there is a peace in meeting your maker because you already know Him, love Him, and work for Him!

So within minutes, my fears turned to faith and I decided to make the foundation a reality in my life. Blessings poured over me so fast, so quickly, so intensely that I spent most of the first year creating the organization with joyful tears in my eyes. My family stepped up to the plate, my friends rallied around me, my co-workers supported events, and my world was peaceful in knowing that I was making a difference because I had answered God's call. I felt elated as we held fundraisers and grew strong as an organization. My parents and Mark believed in me from the beginning. We were officially recognized as a nonprofit.

Many of my friends took on leading roles. Others showed support by attending events and fundraisers. Together, we successfully formed, *A Message of Hope Cancer Fund (MHCF)*. Our mission: to provide direct financial assistance to families who face the monetary burdens associated with cancer. We cover the hidden costs of cancer such as co-pays, prescription drugs, medical equipment, gas to and from treatments, and groceries to promote healthy eating. Within our first year we raised $100,000 and were able to provide true financial relief to those who deserved and needed it the most.

Currently, we are in our second year and I couldn't be happier with the outcome. My friends are remarkable. They've made this organization their own and the fund has become more to them than just wanting to help me; they have experienced the joy that comes from giving. I am so proud of my dear friends for all they have done to grow our organization!

MHCF has meant so much to my own healing. By providing hope to others, I am constantly refreshing my own belief in hope. I'm not giving up or quitting when life is too difficult! By providing hope to others, I feel whole again. I feel healed after facing my own cancer. One of the greatest gifts to date has been the way MHCF has brought people together; uniting them so that they can redefine what it means to have hope in their own lives.

Giving is not always easy! Doing what God calls you to do is not always natural - we are human, right? It's difficult for me at times - sometimes I am selfish, lazy, needy, tired, and complacent! I am a far cry from our great Mother Theresa or our precious Jesus. I am very far from any of those titles. Most days, I'm thrilled that I started such a valuable and purposeful organization. Most days, it is *worth it*. But there are moments where I slip up, get sloppy, and forget about the woman I was meant to be.

I sometimes find myself comparing my efforts to others who are also doing good things in this world. I once felt jealous when I heard about another organization that raised more money faster than we had.

Thankfully, my selfish, moody behavior, which doesn't seem to creep up too often, is just what I need in order to grow with God. In fact, if I were perfect I wouldn't need God. If I was free from sin, free from laziness, or complacency, free from worrying about what other people think, or free from comparing myself to others, I wouldn't need a relationship with Jesus.

Why would I need any higher power in my life if I had it all together all the time? And the truth is none of us have it all together all of the time - no matter how hard we try.

It's been humbling to learn to accept that I'm never free from sin. I'll become selfish and probably fall victim to comparisons again. Each time I sin, I will draw closer to God. He doesn't expect me to be perfect. He brought forgiveness to the world by way of Jesus so that we are always forgiven and given a fresh start. When I surrender (which I do daily), I confess my sins and ask God for forgiveness and guidance. But my intentions are always the same - to serve God by loving people.

By spending time talking to God, in prayer, with all my faults, I release my doubts and fears to Him. Sometimes my prayer is as simple as *God I have been so selfish. I have been so ugly and jealous. I have lost my peace...please help me find it again.* And He always does.

I have noticed that when I feel disconnected from God I am not able to savor life the way I do when I feel close to Him. That's how I know God is leading me in the right direction. It's the feeling of peace versus uneasiness in my soul. When I'm most peaceful and living fully in my top layer, I'm closest to God. I am living for my purpose - humble and giving. When I'm uneasy or easily irritated, I recognize almost instantly that I've forgotten to spend time with God. I've been using my time selfishly.

We all get busy, including me! I don't think God looks at busyness as a sin. We just can't forget our priorities in spite of busyness. And to me, God is priority number one! My plate is full – I'm a reading specialist in a fantastic school. I direct our nonprofit organization. Additionally, Mark and I are raising two beautiful girls. I teach graduate classes, take a few classes towards future career goals, and strive to be an attentive friend! My plate is wonderfully full, but not too full for God. I have discovered that learning about God and building a relationship with Him is well worth the time.

When I take time for my relationship with God, everything else falls into place. I can savor everything on my plate when I'm living my life for God.

And now I am even learning to take time for myself! 1 Corinthians 3:16 says, "Don't you know that you yourselves are God's temple and that God's Spirit lives in you?" So when you're busy fulfilling your daily tasks (including God time), don't forget to take some time out for you! It took me years to figure out how to take time for myself.

At times, I was forced to rest because of illness. Today, I force myself to rest because I want to *avoid* illness. I can't express how important it will be for you to take time to rest, relax, and embrace your daily life in order to achieve your top layer of spirituality.

Now, my dreams for our foundation include continuing to embrace each cancer patient with a spirit of hope; to give them the financial support they need during their fight; to help whoever God puts in our path; and to improve what we as an organization do each day. Personally, I pray about keeping my team, my support system, my incredible family, and my dear friends motivated and connected because without them I can do nothing! The *MHCF* team is a gift from God. The people who help the most (and they know who they are) are the people God sent to provide stability to our organization. I'm certain that He placed in their hearts a desire to make a difference!

Having an all-volunteer organization has been eye opening. I'm blessed to have very dedicated individuals by my side. No one on our team has *the time* for our organization, but our devoted team has made a choice to *make the time*...even when it's difficult. They do it because they're able to feel joy in helping someone other than themselves. It's not always easy for any of us, but as a team we are incredible. Each person takes their role seriously.

We do our best to work smarter so that we can enjoy our work instead of feeling burnt out. We laugh a lot, share our dreams, and emotionally support each other's needs. We divide and conquer, yet unite and prosper. We are in this for the right reasons and to each of us the organization has meant something different.

For me, I know that my cancer had a purpose – a source of hope for someone else. What greater gift could there be than to know that you made a difference in someone's life at a time when *hope* was hard to find?

We've met several amazing families in our journey to share a message of hope. It's been an incredible journey and I know for sure it was a call from God, not my own idea that allowed me to do what I once thought was impossible.

I mentioned in an earlier chapter that I'd purchased a candle at a church fundraiser. The money from the sale of that candle went to help a young girl in need. For many months, Mark and I used this candle while we prayed together. At the time, I thought I'd done a good deed...contributing to help this young girl in her time of need. I later learned that God was setting me up all along to be a part of His grand plan. This little girl had brain cancer and proved to be a source of hope for me during my own fight. She was my hero and I didn't even know her name.

As we planned for our first fundraising gala, we sought nominations from our community to determine which family we'd support first. I was informed that there was one girl, a young precious child, who had been fighting and her mother could really use our help. Soon after meeting Faith Jackson, I made a connection between her story and the story of the young girl I'd heard about at church. I couldn't believe it! I would finally meet the girl who helped me so much. I would finally be able to help her in a way her family needed.

When we met for the first time, we just hugged and cried. Her mother was gracious, in need of our support, and beautiful.

An article about our story was featured in our local newspaper, *The Gazette.*

Wednesday, Feb. 27, 2008

Cancer survivor helps others struggling with disease

Titus Ledbetter III | Staff Writer

Meredith McNerney began lighting a candle and praying for young Faith Jackson in December 2006 when she learned that the Clarksburg child was battling medulloblastoma —

McNerney, a Clarksburg resident, had endured her own operations in August and September of that year to help resolve an inner-ear disorder, known as Meniere's disease, which causes dizziness and can lead to hearing loss.

Then in February 2007, she was diagnosed with a form of skin cancer known as Merkel cell carcinoma.

The cancer was removed and she went through six weeks of radiation last summer. She feels fine these days, but continues to be monitored to make sure the cancer does not return.

Through her own health challenges, McNerney realized that not everyone has the financial means to pay for cancer treatment.

Last month, she founded the nonprofit A Message of Hope Cancer Fund Inc. to raise money to help people battling cancer.

The organization held its first fundraising gala on Feb. 16. The dance, held at Rosensteel Hall of the Knights of Columbus in Silver Spring, drew almost 120 people and raised more than $12,000 — $10,000 of which will go to Faith and her family, who McNerney met for the first time in December.

McNerney first heard about Faith's story after buying a candle from St. Paul's Catholic Church in Damascus to support the girl and her family. Faith's mother, Katie Jackson, had to stop working to take care of her daughter.

"Faith brought so much inspiration every time I lit that candle," McNerney said. "I would think about her before I knew who she was. She really had no idea how much of an inspiration she was to me. There were many nights once I was diagnosed with cancer that I would continue to light that candle, pray with my husband, and think about her. To be able to give back is so rewarding for me."

The first goal of the new cancer fund is to provide 10 families with an average gift of $10,000 in 2008. The organization serves people in Maryland, but McNerney would like to expand it to Virginia and Washington, D.C., before stretching across the country.

Faith was diagnosed with medulloblastoma on Dec. 9, 2005. She underwent a nine-hour surgery at Children's National Medical Center in Washington, D.C., to remove the tumor and stayed in the hospital

until Dec. 27. Then she spent a month in
rehabilitation.

She did not attend classes during the 2005-2006
school year because she had to regain her strength.
However, she returned to school part-time as a Rocky
Hill Middle School sixth-grader in the fall of 2006 and
became in full-time seventh-grader last fall. She
finished her chemotherapy last summer.

Faith, now 12, attended the fundraising event earlier
this month with her mother and her sister Kayla, 14.

"I thought it was a lot of fun because I was there with
my family," Faith said. "We don't really get to spend a
lot of time just us together. It was fun to dance with my
sister and my Mom."

Katie Jackson said it was great to see how much
support McNerney and her organization received. She
said she appreciates the monetary gift, which she
would use to help pay bills and get back on her feet.

"You meet people every day, but you don't meet
people like Meredith every day — somebody who is
positive and encouraging and very giving," Jackson
said. "It is really her heart that is giving back out of
everything she has experienced. I think that she is a
wonderful person."

Jackson said that Faith is doing much better, but she
still has some nerve damage to her legs as a result of
the chemotherapy. While Faith has faced emotional
challenges since she has gone back to school full-time,
Katie Jackson said she appreciates the support the
family has received from the Clarksburg community.

"As a single mom having two daughters, it has been a
very difficult position to be in," Jackson said. "I'm

extremely grateful from the bottom of my heart for all of the people. All Faith's teachers and the staff at her school have been amazing. All of the people that have supported us have really helped us."

McNerney said that A Message of Hope Cancer Fund also has a team of lawyers to investigate the families to whom her organization provides financial help to make sure that scam artists do not receive funds.

She credits her family and friends for helping to put together the organization's first fundraiser in only six weeks.

"My friends and family have rallied around me even when I was unsure of the idea just to say that they loved me and they supported me and that they would walk the journey with me," McNerney said.

"Every person that has helped out truly believes that this will be a huge organization one day and that we will have the ability to help so many families."

I was so thrilled when the article was published on the front page of our local newspaper because to me it was an even greater confirmation that we were moving in the right direction. I knew the organization would become what God wanted it to be!

Below is one example of the type of letters we receive from the families we've helped. When I need hope, I read the letters to stay positive. They serve as a reminder that life is all about loving God, yourself, and your neighbor.

Faith's mom shares her heart in support of our organization.

My name is Katie Jackson. I am a single mom with two daughters, Kayla age 15 and Faith age 13. It was

Wednesday, December 7, 2005 when my youngest daughter, Faith, was diagnosed with Medulloblastoma – a cancerous brain tumor.

Faith was a happy, healthy 5th grader about to turn 11 years old. There are no words to express the grief that comes over you. This is your child – you want them to be OK. I remember like it was only yesterday. I thought Faith had the flu.

I had decided to take her to the emergency room. After initial tests we were then transported to Children's National Medical Center in Washington, D.C. where Faith was admitted and I was told Faith had what they thought was to be a cancerous brain tumor.

She needed surgery immediately – it was scheduled for the following day. The surgery lasted all day and Faith was transferred to the ICU and five days later to a regular room where she would recover. The neurosurgeon said, "This is the beginning of a long road." He was right. Our lives were forever changed. Nothing would ever be the same.

You start to wonder how you're going to manage and how you will make it through. What about my job? What about my bills? What is going to happen to my daughter? Faith was in the hospital for two months following her surgery. She spent one month at Children's Hospital and then was transferred to a rehabilitation hospital for one month. Faith started cancer treatment while she was still in the hospital. She had six weeks of radiation and 13 months of chemotherapy.

Faith is now in remission and continues to make progress. Faith still has weekly doctor's appointments to maintain and many medical challenges to overcome. She is getting stronger daily. Although Faith is in the process of recovery we are still left with the aftermath of the storm. No one can be prepared for the financial burden cancer places on a family.

In December 2007, two years into the difficult journey I received a phone call from *A Message of Hope Cancer Fund* asking to sponsor our family in a fundraising event. When I received this message all I could do was cry. It was an answer to a prayer. *A Message of Hope* is "a message of hope" bringing hope to families who have nothing left to hold on to – families who are on this long journey and are tired and have no place to turn.

Once I had a chance to meet and talk with the people and volunteers at *A Message of Hope Cancer Fund*, I immediately felt connected like we had known each other our whole lives. Each volunteer has a story and a reason for being there – a caring and giving heart and a passion to help others. I know firsthand they will do just that.

A Message of Hope Cancer Fund was able to offer me financial relief so my burdens were lighter. I was amazed at the goodness of people working with *A Message of Hope*. I have a renewed sense of good in mankind and am forever thankful to them.

Katie Jackson

It was a call from God and I'm grateful that He woke me on that cold November morning. Each day I am humbled in knowing that I trusted Him enough to listen.

The gift of purpose for me came as a result of having faced cancer. Without going through it myself, I know I wouldn't have felt called to start something so important. I look at my cancer as a gift and I thank God for continuing to see me through the battle.

I was thrilled with all that had been accomplished, but I often heard a quiet whisper telling me it was time to take care of my own needs, and then there was the nagging reminder of how much pain I was experiencing on the left side of my face. I began to think seriously about facing the reconstructive process. It was finally time to move forward and approach the next phase of my healing.

14

FORGIVENESS

*The Lord helps me! Why should I be afraid of what people
can do to me?"*
Hebrews 13:6

Have you ever cried a deep, dark cry? A cry of despair when
you think everything has fallen apart. A cry in which you
recognize that you can't handle where life has you at the
moment and you're sad and angry for all you've been
through?

I finally cried like that.

For me, it was two weeks after my first reconstructive surgery.
It wasn't that I didn't want to cry, it was that I just hadn't let
myself.

The first surgery left my face looking worse than it did before.
As expected, plastic reconstructive surgery of the face comes
with a long recovery. I didn't want to cry because I wanted to
be strong, but I felt like a train-wreck.

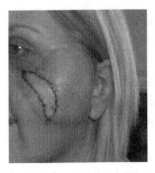

It looked as if I'd been in an
accident and the recovery was tough.
A few nights before my melt down,
Mark came up to the guest bedroom
where I was resting to check on me.
I was home from the hospital after
being there for five long days. My
face was swollen, bruised, and
unattractive.

As you now know, during the previous surgeries doctors cut nerves, blood vessels, tissue, and fat down to the bone. Now the goal was to rebuild my face and "fill in" the missing parts. It was decided that the best place to take the needed "parts" would be from my arm. This would require a skin graft. A skin graft is when a patch of skin is removed by surgery from one area of the body and transplanted, or attached, to another area.

To my surprise, not a piece, but a section of fat, tissue, blood vessels and nerves that measured nearly 3 inches wide and almost 6 inches long was taken from my arm. My arm looked badly burned and it was extremely painful. Additionally, both of my hips were cut, using the skin from my hips to cover the chunk taken from my arm.

I was in bad shape and began wondering why I ever went through with this surgery. As Mark came to see me that evening he said something that I needed to hear.

"It's okay to cry, you know."

"I know," I said as my eyes began to swell. "I know."

"You don't have to be so strong all the time. You deserve to be angry for once. I don't expect you to be so positive all the time. No one expects that of you," he said gently.

I nodded my head and reached for a hug. He was right, but I wasn't ready. I needed to remain strong to get through it. I needed to be tough to heal.

The surgery was in some ways my choice. Obviously I wasn't going to die without it. This was about closure. I needed to move forward. I didn't want to look in the mirror every day and see the aftermath of cancer. It's not that I was uncomfortable with my appearance. I had come too far in my journey to be uncomfortable with any part of who I was. I wanted the closure. I wanted to move forward. I needed the finality of it all.

Most importantly I needed the surgery to help alleviate the pain. I couldn't be touched without feeling pain on the left side of my face. My face was so raw and would never heal without surgery. There was no protection and I nearly fainted each time accidental contact was made to the left side of my face. It was that type of contact that became a reminder of why I wanted my face put back together.

On the morning of the surgery, I felt calm. My father and Mark drove me to the hospital where we arrived at 6 a.m. It was cold and dark outside, but I felt safe and was hardly nervous. The doctor looked over my face, again. He searched my body trying to determine the best place to take the needed tissue, nerves, and blood vessels.

The surgery wasn't a guarantee. It was possible that the necessary parts would *die* in the transfer. After deliberating, he selected my arm. He felt that taking what he needed from my arm would give me the best chance at a successful surgery.

"Which hand do you write with, Meredith?" the doctor asked.

"My left," I cheerfully replied.

So he felt, listened, and determined which sections he would cut. He marked my face and arm - everything was in place to start on time.

As the nurse wheeled me down to the OR, I remember hugging and kissing my father and husband. They both felt warm and comforting to me. My mom was at home getting the girls off to school, but soon the three of them would be waiting at the hospital to support me during the entire surgery.

We entered the OR and I began to shiver just a bit. It was very cold and the nurses quickly wrapped me in extra blankets. Lying flat, I was still and started to feel a little nervous. I prayed over and over *I can do all things through Christ who strengthens me.* I stared at the ceiling - my eyes focused on how unfinished it was, unpainted, sterile, and cold, but extremely bright – keeping my mind off of why I was really there.

Doctors were preparing. The room was loud and I sensed a busyness surrounding me. Prayer kept me calm. I let go of the control and began to relax and trust in the people who were there to care for me. To my surprise, a man came over just to hold my hand. I held his hand back and felt comforted. *He's a true example of loving your neighbor. You're a stranger to me, but somehow I feel connected to you.*

The doctors asked me simple questions, like "Who brought you here this morning?" and "Where are you from?" (The funny little games they play to see if you are still coherent). Smiling back at them, I was keenly aware of my relaxed state. I was drifting off slowly. *I've done this before. I am ready.*

The surgery lasted nine hours. My family stayed the entire time. I woke up feeling groggy, but somewhat coherent. My left eye was swollen shut which irritated me, but I was tired more than anything and glad it was over.

The nurse was careful to administer my pain medication on time and I was peaceful. For most of the evening I slept and let time pass.

And then, intense pain ripped through me and my once peaceful sleep was interrupted. Aggressive pressure. Anguish. Torment. Sorrow. My head was pounding.

A new nurse started the morning shift and I quickly realized she hadn't administered my pain medication on time. I asked for relief from my headache as it started to become unbearable. I could deal with my face, arm, and hips, but my head was excruciating.

The pain ran from my chin all the way up my face, to the back of my head, down my neck, and into my shoulders.

Not sure what else to do, I began to beg for help. I was crying out, but was ignored. Finally, the nurse came and admitted she didn't give me the pain medicine because I hadn't asked for it. She assumed since I was sleeping that I was feeling fine. I couldn't believe someone caring for a patient after major surgery could be so careless. Letting the pain get out of control and then trying to treat it meant that it would take much longer to control it again.

I was angry. As she injected medication into my IV, I held onto hope...but there was minimal relief in sight. My head was throbbing and I was still – waiting for the doctor to arrive.

When the doctor witnessed the agonizing discomfort I was in, he immediately ordered an anti-inflammatory to reduce the swelling that had engulfed me. Finally, the remedy I needed! My family came to visit and I felt peaceful. I was happy I'd made it this far. I wanted to heal, to be able to move forward, to be positive.

But my harmonious state was abruptly stripped away, again. As one nurse left her shift and another took over, one of them made a huge mistake while recording the dosing of my pain medication. I knew for sure that the medication the doctor prescribed had worked. Of course, I was receiving pain medication for my face, arm and hips, but I needed that additional dose that specifically got rid of my massive migraine headache. The dosing was recorded wrong. I was to receive 30 milligrams of medication every six hours. I knew that I had received a dose at 4 p.m. It provided relief and I was grateful.

I was certain from my experience the night before that I needed to be an advocate for myself in order to receive all medication on time. And that's exactly what I did. At 8 p.m. that evening, I began to remind the nurse that I would need a dose of medication at 10 p.m. She became agitated, but assured me that I would receive my medication on time. At 10 p.m. I hit the call button to ask for the drugs.

My head was pounding once again. I felt the medication wearing off like a protective mask slowly peeling away – leaving me raw and in pain once again. Tense tears filled my eyes. I called the nurse once again and no one came. Each time, someone who answered the call button assured me that they would tell my nurse that I was in pain.

Why was I being ignored? Who was to blame? I didn't care if I was annoying! My head was pounding. Why didn't anyone want to help me? Finally, forty-five minutes later, the nurse came to tell me that I was not getting the medication until midnight.

"No!" I corrected her. "I am to have this medication every six hours. I'm certain that's what the doctor ordered."

She looked at my chart where the dosing was recorded incorrectly and seemed confused.

"I'm not sure why it says a dose of 15 milligrams every eight hours," she seemed puzzled. "The last dose says 30 milligrams, but it looks like someone wrote something different for the next dose."

Okay, it's a mistake. Fine, just fix it. "Can you please fix the dose and take care of me?"

"Well, no," she admitted with an attitude, "I can't just change the dose."

The pain was escalating and I started to shiver. "Please help me, I am in pain, I am shaking, and I need help."

"I will try to call someone," she rolled her eyes and left.

I was losing control of my body. My body shook uncontrollably – even my lips quivered.

"I want the head nurse," I demanded as I yelled into the call button.

"I need someone to take me seriously," I tried to stick up for myself.

"I need blankets! I am freezing! I need help! Please stop ignoring me!"

With an irritated stare back at me, as if I was exaggerating, two blankets were tossed over me to shut me up for the moment. I couldn't believe the lack of care. *This is a nightmare.*

I would have given anything to have my face ripped off and to cancel the whole surgery. I wanted it to be over. *How could this be happening to me, again? What have I done, Lord, to deserve this type of punishment?* I couldn't think clearly or rationally at this point. No one was helping me. No one cared. My thoughts were crazed and I hated everything at that moment.

This is so unfair...I do not deserve this at all.

Finally, I was given a few more blankets and the shivering stopped. The blankets provided the warmth that I needed to calm down.

Lord, I am so pissed off right now. Many, many inappropriate words raced through my mind. It took everything in me to even *want* to pray. Helpless and lost, I began to pray my own version of the Jabez prayer. *Bless me, oh Lord, indeed. Expand my territory to include goodness. Have your hand in all that I do and protect me from evil.* The prayer ran through my mind repeatedly - protecting my soul from the evil images and horrific thoughts that once filled my spirit.

The pain was still unbearable, but as I prayed I felt a sense of peace within that reminded me that I would make it through this tribulation. The nurse returned to tell me that she could not fix the dosing until the morning because she could not reach the doctor until then, but that she could give me another pain medication on top of what I was receiving every hour if I requested it. Of course, I found it difficult to rest, or sleep, or let my guard down. If I dozed off, she would forget about me and I couldn't let that happen. I had to be an advocate for myself and never let the pain get so out of control.

Finally, after what felt like days, with time passing slower than I ever remembered before, the doctor returned to learn about what happened the previous night. I don't really know what he said to the staff, but after that I received the best care possible for the next three days of my hospital stay.

A new shift brought about pleasant changes. Nurses gave me the correct doses of medication and gave me the medication on time. They smiled back at me and I was able to rest and recover.

On the last night in the hospital, I was moved to a less critical floor. After the horrifying experience a few nights before, I was afraid to move. I was finally receiving excellent care and the nurses who had been taking such good care of me were scheduled to work the next few shifts. I knew them and I didn't want to leave. I was nervous to start all over again.

I prayed fervently that my God would protect me. I asked for nurses who would be attentive to my needs and administer correct amounts of medication. This was all I ever wanted.

God answered my prayers the moment I arrived on my new floor. My nurse was jovial and kind. I explained what had happened and she said something that I wish was true of every nurse in every hospital.

"Don't worry, honey. I'm not here for the paycheck. I'm here because I want to help people like you. This is my calling, so don't you worry!"

Profuse tears filled my eyes. I knew she was a gift from God. She provided me comfort and even asked if I would like her to pray with me. We prayed and then I truly rested. When her shift ended, I felt ready for whatever was ahead. She provided me peace through our common relationship with Jesus Christ. She gave me a renewed gift.

The next nurse was also helpful and she even thanked *me* for being so appreciative of her. I was glad to offer praise for a job well done. I always try to be the first person to offer praise when someone deserves it. Many nurses are excellent, underpaid, and underappreciated. To them, I am grateful.

During my ordeal, I reflected about God and fairness. Sometimes life just seems unfair. Sometimes people harm others out of hate. I wondered why our society is filled with uncaring, rude people. I wondered why some nurses were so much more conscientious than others.

I prayed that God would help me understand why more people in this world are not as kind as they should be. The negligent nurses were not in tune with what God had called them to do. They were not acting in faith – they freely made this choice. I know God felt my pain and understood how I was feeling. Sometimes I wonder how hurt God must be when He witnesses the bad choices His people make.

Obviously we all have choices and many people are selfish, self-centered, lazy, and unreliable. We can't get mad at God when people choose this type of behavior. We must instead work with God to find peace when dealing with such people. In turn, we must act in a manner that reflects God's plan for our lives. His plan is not only revealed in our divine purpose, but in our daily experiences.

In prayer, I learned to forgive those nurses and release the bitterness I carried towards them. With God's support, I realized that I was holding on to the pain, thus deepening my anger and consequently I was unable to move forward peacefully. By forgiving someone for their actions you are not excusing their behavior, but instead releasing the hurt and allowing yourself to heal.

What keeps me motivated in following God are my beliefs about will. Acting in God's will or according to His plan doesn't mean you will be spared the heartache or pain of dealing with people who hurt you. However, the gifts that come out of following God's plan include forgiveness, peace, purpose, fulfillment, and love. He will help you deal with all of the awful experiences we encounter on earth and one day when you live an eternal life in heaven, you will never again have to deal with selfish people who are only concerned with themselves.

I think that's why it took me so long to ever really cry after my first reconstructive surgery. Like my husband said, "You deserve to be angry or mad." Yes, I deserved it, but I wasn't going to act on it out of anger. I was feeling so peaceful and calm, rested, and ready to recover.

But two weeks later, the exhausted human part of me took over and I started feeling sorry for myself. I should have surrendered to God and prayed over those feelings, but I just didn't want to. I wanted to sulk, feel sorry for myself, and resent my story just to see what it felt like. I had been so positive, but I needed to let go of that positive energy for a moment to feel hurt for all that I had been through. I gave in to this temptation willingly.

In my own bed I sobbed like a baby. I created a pile of tears to remind myself how unfair my life had been. I told myself that I didn't deserve any of this and that I should be angry for all I'd been through. Bitterness and hostility had a hold of me.

For the last three years I've had to endure such heartache. Why me? I'm a faithful person. I love God. Why am I going through this torture? Life sucks. And this is unfair. I am angry and pissed off. God promised me good would come of this – where is the good? Nothing makes cancer "worth it." Even the good from my foundation doesn't make cancer "worth it." Life is too difficult and I'm not okay with it all.

Thirty minutes later I realized that feeling sorry for myself, although it did feel good for a while, was getting me nowhere. I'd seen many good things come as a result of my pain, but once again, God assured me that He wasn't finished revealing His plan to me. I envisioned more blessings ahead – I needed to be ready for them. If I spent my time sulking and feeling sorry for myself, then I would miss what God had in store for me. His timing is perfect and although I'd like to be finished with life's hard stuff, I'm far from done. I soon remembered that God would be with me along the way.

Life is full of temptations – beckoning me to act selfishly and give up my relationship with God. But worldly temptations are too weak in the power of God. There's nothing in or out of this world that could possibly fulfill me the way my God does.

Too often, I meet people who believe God has punished them in some way for the sins in their lives. They regretfully miss the lessons and the opportunities to know God because they have misinterpreted His love. When God lives in your heart, you understand His ability to forgive you and love you unconditionally.

I often make mistakes, move off course, and sin. The beauty of the relationship I have with God is that I know without a doubt if I admit my sins to Him and ask for forgiveness, He will forgive me. Admitting my mistakes has helped me to follow God's plan for my life. Admitting when I am wrong has shaped me into a better person. I want to teach my children how to admit when they are wrong, accept responsibility and fully experience God's forgiveness.

My daughter, Danielle, recently did something that she later felt ashamed of. I was really upset with her and wanted to yell, say hurtful things, and send her away to her room. But I stopped myself. I realized that she knew she was wrong. She was hurting because she felt embarrassed for what she had done...she felt shameful. I pray that I can be the type of mother God has called me to be. Again, the same simple lesson rings true- "Treat your neighbor as you want to be treated." Of course this means our children, too!

I know shame. I have felt shame before. I knew by yelling at her and sending her to her room, I would deepen her shame and send a message that said, YOU ARE NOT WORTHY OF MY LOVE AT THE MOMENT.

Instead I refocused, took a deep breath, and asked her to join me in my room. As we lay in bed together, she cried, dug her head in the pillow, and felt shame. I asked her to confess what she did, although I already knew. At first she began to blame, to pass the responsibility, to hide from the truth. I reminded her that she would be forgiven, but only when she committed to personal responsibility and became truthful about what she had done. She openly shared, with tears and embarrassment. We talked about how she felt. I listened and held her. She cried and began to really seek forgiveness. We prayed.

With my hand on her chest, I felt her heart racing nervously. Together we asked Jesus to forgive her actions and I reinforced forgiveness by letting her know that I also forgave her. Quickly her heartbeat calmed and I watched as she accepted forgiveness and gained peace again. She witnessed God's love instead of continuing to carry shame in her heart.

In that moment, I felt strongly that her suffering could be used to teach her a lesson and build her character. Just as God wants to do with each of us, I wanted to shape her, mold her, and guide her into being a better, more peaceful person. It was a lesson I knew she would learn if I took the time to teach her. These lessons are always valuable. God is not punishing us; He is teaching out of love and shaping us to build our character. I feel proud of who I am when I treat my children in a way that makes God proud.

I realize that people, especially young people, need someone to demonstrate forgiveness. It is my hope that I'm that person to my daughters. I want them to understand God, His love, and His forgiveness by modeling unconditional love to them.

Today, I continue to read more, ask more questions, and learn more every day of my life. I understand forgiveness and love. I am committed to remaining focused on God's will to be an example to my children and help them to fully fall in love with God. Just as I've educated myself about so many other important topics in life, I'm grateful for the knowledge that I've gained as a result of studying God. I crave to learn more of God's word and will spend the rest of my life studying Him!

And in the end, what I realize the most about forgiveness is that you cannot fully receive it or give it if you haven't learned to forgive yourself for the times you've failed. After creating a mess of tears in my bed that day, I decided to forgive myself. I'd been angry and although I deserved to be mad at the world, my pain was only fully healed when I embraced my journey with a loving heart. At the moment I decided to savor life again and fully embrace forgiveness on all levels, I found myself truly living...once again.

15

YOU

My dear friends, we must love each other. Love comes from God, and when we love each other, it shows that we have been given new life. We are now God's children, and we know him.

1 John 4:7

Above all, this book is a gift for my daughters. At the most unexpected times, I am reminded of my own daughters' feelings about cancer. Danielle came home from Kindergarten one day and brought tears to my eyes after she shared her perspective on cancer. After the first reconstructive surgery, she wrote her own book about my journey.

My Mom Has Cancer
Illustrated by Danielle

My Mom has been going
through a lot of cancer

But I think she looks pretty

My Mom will be back to normal soon

My Mom is normal

I love my Mom

I love that she thinks I am *pretty* and *normal.* I'm certain she will change her mind when she is a teenager, but for now I am enjoying her loving perspective of me! Both of my daughters inspire me to remain positive.

While writing, I began to realize that so many *good* people were questioning their own faith. It was as if I kept hearing the same story, but from different people. From most I heard, "I am questioning my faith right now. I believe there must be something greater, a higher power, but I don't know what I really believe. I feel a void in my life that I am unable to fill. I just think that so many people who say they are Christians are the same people who are rude, hostile, and judgmental. It's hard to have hope."

It was as if God intended for this to happen – for me to hear these same comments over and over and motivate me to share my story publicly. And so I became inspired to share my perspective.

I believe that all people want peace in their lives. I think if we were a happier, more peaceful society, we could cope more positively with many of life's problems and hardships. Each day we experience rudeness, jealousy, unhealthy competition, and greed.

People today, as a society, have more than ever before. Our houses are bigger than our parents' were, our cars are fancier and more luxurious, we crave extravagant vacations, and we are typically ungrateful as we seek more, and more, and more! In our quietest, darkest moments, there is a void; a loss of self. Emptiness fills us and we think that if we add more "stuff," we can be fulfilled. At the same time, our faith is tested over and over again. Then, because of our own pain and insecurities, we begin to lose faith in each other and lose sight of living the way God intended us to live – with love for one another. Our relationships break down and we are left feeling empty, once again. More often, we begin to judge one another, make harsh comparisons, or simply lose the spirit which guides us to give and receive love. But remember, that while you are experiencing this pain, God is waiting for you to surrender to Him – to release your void and let Him fill it.

I love the scripture according to Luke 6:37 – "Do not judge and you will not be judged. Do not condemn, and you will not be condemned." People tend to judge each other based on religious beliefs, job status, material possessions, and even motherhood. When it comes to religion I don't believe in a lot of complicated rules or competition. I believe in God. I believe in forgiveness. I believe in love. I believe in peace. I believe deep in my heart that God is not complicated at all.

Sometimes we cannot understand the world, but God understands us. God is love.

I believe that our judgment against each other causes intolerance and promotes division. I believe in a God that promotes unity, tolerance, and love. Our whole world is full of judgment, but my journey has taught me to judge less and love more.

I believe in creating an authentic relationship with God by worshiping Him in a way that is based on true love. An example of this can be found at church. Many people attend church each week out of obligation because they believe the "rulebook of life" says you should go, that you are wrong or sinful if you do not attend. But church is not a competition like many other parts of our lives; we should attend church because we want to be there to learn, to listen, and to grow. When we start "doing God" out of obligation, we fail to learn anything. Some people just want the gold star for attendance, the bragging rights. We all know a few people who feel it's necessary to let everyone know that they never miss a Sunday service, yet on the other hand they are full of gossip and judgment on Monday morning. Poor examples of "Christians" are all around us. We are negatively influenced by the people who attend church each week and walk out the door only to slide back into the "real world." They fall right back into their pattern of being rude and hurtful.

Some families fight about what to wear before church, fight in the car on the ride to church, smile and look peaceful while they are there, and then come home only to fight about money, bills, or the stressors related to the week ahead. We are all human, but to be true examples of Christ we have to be willing to become more authentic in our relationship with God and each other.

While deepening my authentic relationship with God, church offers me a place to worship and learn with fellow believers. This fosters peace within my heart. However, it's through my own willingness and commitment to seek peace ALL week, that I'm able to benefit from organized worship service on Sunday.

If you feel the need, I hope you will discover your own deeper relationship and begin to understand how much God wants to be a part of your life.

But many wonder why such a loving God allows us to suffer. Suffering is a part of life. God never promised a life without suffering. According to Matthew 16:24-26, "If any of you want to be my followers, you must forget about yourself. You must take up your cross and follow me. If you want to save your life, you will destroy it. But if you give up your life for me, you will find it. What will you gain, if you own the whole world but destroy yourself? What would you give to get back your soul?"

Jesus wants us to empty ourselves so that God can fill us. When we suffer, we can choose to seek consolation in Jesus and become closer to God. And then we will learn of the most beautiful peace that surpasses all understanding.

Only in eternal life will we be removed from suffering, illness, surgery, death, pain, violence, trauma, or heartache. It is in our life on earth, a blink in time when compared to eternal life, that we come to know God. It is by our own pain and suffering that we learn about God's love for us. Remember that God is our heavenly father and just like a human parent, God wants to console us, love us, lift us up, and give us strength when we suffer.

By understanding that life on earth is not at all like eternal life, it becomes apparent that we will all experience some form of suffering. Many create unnecessary suffering by choosing to live life with a negative perspective. That is self-created suffering. But we must be smart enough to draw the line between real suffering and unnecessary worry. My relationship with God allows me to release my suffering. I would not, and do not, allow myself to believe negative thoughts or live with unreal worry. If I worry, and I do because I'm human, I almost immediately turn that worry over to God. I realize that worry creates stress and stress creates illness. God is ready to help all of us – no matter how small or large the problem may seem – but we must be willing to accept His loving support.

However, even the most positive, hope-filled people will endure hardship. If you are currently battling a serious illness, I understand the complicated emotional path that you must be facing. As you now know, I have walked down a path where illness controlled my life. If you are experiencing emotional or physical pain, I first want you to know that I am praying for you. I'm praying that you will be honest with yourself about how you feel, careful enough to surround yourself with people who deeply support you, and wise enough to seek professional help if you need it.

Suffering can be a part of all aspects of life. That doesn't mean that we aren't meant to savor life. Many mothers suffer to balance work and career – so do I. Some of my friends suffer to make their marriages work. Many people suffer over money or temptation or the mundane parts of life. Of course we suffer over bigger issues such as death, pain, illness and so on. I look at suffering as a way to draw closer to God. I accepted my suffering and surrendered it to God.

And the beauty of suffering is that with each hardship, there is a lesson. With each pain, there is a light that allows you to remain peaceful. With each tragedy, there is a new way of viewing life. It is up to you to choose your own path to peacefulness.

You have to seek peace as an option. All too often, when faced with difficulties, people want to blame. It's only natural to want to blame God. But when my life was too difficult to handle on my own, God was my only hope to finding peace.

My goal was to share my darkest days, my deepest hurts, and my pain to help you realize that you're not alone. God is ready and waiting to build a relationship with you that provides you hope in a way that you have never experienced before. I have walked the journey from pain to peace over and over again, but my journey is far from over. However, I know for sure, God will never let me walk alone.

When I am in need of a positive message, I hope to look back at all I have endured and realize that life is always worth living and that each day is a gift. This is a message of hope for me, my daughters, my family, my friends, and for you. I hope my trials will help you face your pain with greater ease.

It is my hope that we will all learn how to survive our most difficult pain. Learning to survive difficult times is more than just surviving – it's learning to live life to the fullest. It's deciding that you are not willing to give in. As a survivor, you can redefine your life and confidently embrace it with a purpose. We start the process by **searching** for God and becoming willing to let Him become a part of our pain. Then, true survivors begin to live with the *hope* that there is a great purpose to all **suffering**. At the point in which we are able to **surrender** our suffering to God, is the moment we begin to build a life worth **savoring.**

Embrace your journey with a spirit of hope, and as the serenity prayers says, learn to accept what you cannot change and be courageous enough to change what you can. I challenge you to be the strong one.

Along the way the process will get messy. At times you may lose yourself, slip away, and feel a need to search again. For me, this is an on-going process; one where I find myself moving through each layer during different challenges in my life – but my peace is easily restored in prayer. It's only when I forget, and I fail to remember the power that is present in my relationship with God, that I become uneasy and worry fills my soul. In prayer, I am healed once again and ready to savor life with a grateful spirit.

If you've read this far, I pray that my story has influenced you in a positive way. If my story has made a difference to you, then my battles have had a purpose. I pray for peace, patience, and faith in your life. And most importantly, I pray that you will begin a new or renewed relationship with your heavenly father who loves you so much.

Go and build your own spiritual layers of the sweetest, most fulfilling cake that authentically allows you to embrace who God created you to be.

And may He bless you every step of the way.

EPILOGUE

As of summer 2009, I am feeling fantastic and fully recovered from cancer. I am constantly monitored with body scans and periodic CT scans. Additionally, my face has undergone two reconstructive surgeries – the second which was not discussed in the book was very easy to recover from – and a third is planned. I am no longer in pain as a result of the reconstruction and overall I am pleased with the outcome.

More often than I'd like, I deal with episodes of vertigo but each time I am reminded of how much I desire the opportunity to help those who also suffer.

After working with a researcher in the field of dermatology, I recently learned that I have a predisposition to cancer. This discovery began when I tested positive for the Polyomavirus. The Polyomavirus is often linked to Merkel Cell and is present in most patients with the disease. At the same time, I am learning that due to a gene mutation, I do not have the proper immune system to reject the virus. While most people will never be affected by the virus, for some genetic reason I do not produce the antibodies against it. Now doctors are trying to find the gene in my DNA that is responsible for all of my health issues – a genetic mutation or flaw.

Once the gene has been identified, doctors can use the information to determine if a person is predisposed to certain skin cancers. This new research has the potential to be groundbreaking and could affect generations to come. For now, I pray for the team of doctors who are hoping to make these discoveries and although my journey has been tough, it would be fascinating to know that my struggles led to the discovery of something that could help future generations.

I was alone recently. Driving. Listening to my favorite Christian radio station (WTGS, 91.9) and thinking.

I am finally in a place where I think I was always meant to be...a healthy place both physically and spiritually. And as my eyes burned with tears, I told God that I was ready – ready for the next part of His perfectly created plan.

And with that I felt free.

Before Cancer

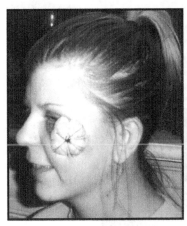
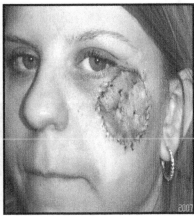

March 7, 2007   March 15, 2007

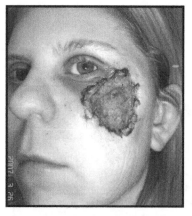

March 26, 2007

April 3, 2007

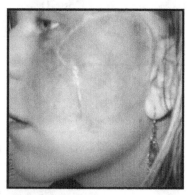

May 5, 2007

Summer 2007

February 2008

Our Family
November 2008

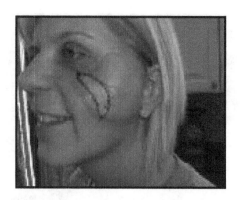

First Reconstructive Surgery
December 2008

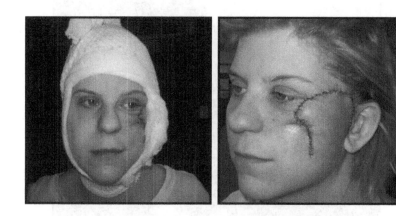

Second Reconstructive Surgery – April 2009

Without make-up!
June 2009

My parents with our family
June 2009

DEDICATION

Mothers and Daughters

Dear Danielle and Kaitlyn,

I still tear up every time I allow myself to think about life had I not survived cancer. I often think how grateful I am to be alive...to laugh with both of you, play chase, read books, bake, and make a mess together.

I want so badly to share my heart with you, to find the right words to express my feelings, but I have tried to write this message many times and have struggled to find the words. Even now, as I attempt this difficult dedication, I am emotional. I'm not sure how to fully express how much you both mean to me.

I believe the greatest gift I can give to either of you is my love. Your father and I could not imagine our lives without our precious girls. It is my hope that the love your daddy and I share for each other can be an example to both of you. He is such an incredible husband to me and I pray that one day both of you will fall in love with someone who supports and loves you as much as your father has loved me.

It may be difficult to read, but I want to share how much your love meant to me during my battle with cancer. First, I want to remind you that when I was diagnosed, Danielle you were 4 years old, and Kaitlyn you were only 2 years old. I am grateful that you were so young. You were both such spirited, happy children, and you helped me stay positive.

Raising young children requires a lot of attention and although some days it was difficult to have the energy I needed to take care of both of you, I was never alone. Your dad was always involved in supporting me and spending time with both of you. When I really needed a break, he would take you to your favorite place to get a donut, or run in the backyard with you or take you to a local park. He was smart enough to give me the time I needed to rest, in a quiet house! At the same time, I wanted you both to feel secure in my health and I never wanted you to think I was "sick."

Although my appearance changed quite a bit, neither of you ever seemed to know when things were really bad. Your innocence was calming for me.

I want to help you remember how kind you were as I endured each facial surgery and my appearance begin to change dramatically! After the first surgery, I came home with a massive bandage sewn to my face. It was yellow in color and shaped like a large piece of cauliflower. You both were so excited to see me when I came home, that you just smiled and laughed a little at the cauliflower. You were never scared or fearful. You both embraced me with hugs and wanted me to play a game right away.

I am not sure at that point that either of you had heard the word "cancer," but you did not question my appearance very much. Life went on normally for both of you. After each surgery, I was bandaged and bruised. At one point, I had black stitches across the entire left half of my face. Only once, Kaitlyn, did you mention that you didn't like "mommy's boo-boo," but both of you girls quickly forgot. I just kept smiling.

Once my face healed from the radiation, I was left with a large scar, but neither of you seemed to notice. Then as I faced reconstruction, you were only thrilled when I came home, even though I looked "funny." With a smile on my swollen face, I told you that it would be OK if you teased me a little and called me "chipmunk" – as my face was so swollen. I wanted you to witness my sense of humor about it all. I truly believe that you both felt loved and that was all that seemed to matter.

I am grateful to the many family members and friends who supported our family during such a difficult time. I remember soon after I battled cancer, I called your Aunt Ronya with a heavy heart, full of fear. Even though I often felt strong and positive during my fight, there were moments when I'd think about the future and would just fall apart! I needed her to reassure me that if anything were to ever happen to me that she would play a large role in your lives. She adores both of you. Even though she never doubted that I would be able to beat cancer, she did what I needed and offered her support.

I had several hard days when I would think about the "what ifs?" and worry. I never worried about death itself, but I worried about what I would miss if I died too young. I trusted that your father, grandparents, aunts and uncles would be amazing to both of you, but I was not ready to watch over you from heaven. I was determined to fight with hope because of both of you. In time, I learned to trust God and worry less.

Sometimes, even now, I cannot help but to wonder what would happen if I had cancer again. I do not fear cancer anymore because I have learned that in the bible we are reminded 365 times to "Fear Not!" I feel peace today about my health. It is not a fear anymore, but when my mind wanders, I begin to pray. I have talked to God many times about how much I want to take part in your lives and have asked Him to keep us all safe. When I begin to think about facing cancer again, I quickly pray and find peace in knowing that His plan for each of us is perfect.

My hope is that you will both continue your relationship with Jesus and that you will grow into an even greater friendship with Him. I pray for you each night to feel the power of the Holy Spirit within your souls and know how much you are loved.

Watching you both grow into such precious young girls has been so rewarding for your father and me. Many nights after you are asleep, we talk about how much you both mean to us. Often we comment on just how adorable you both are, how funny you are when you play together, and how grateful we are to be your parents. We have our moments, don't get me wrong, when parenting is not easy, but I have to say that we love you more and more each day.

Thank you for giving me the strength to face cancer with hope. I love you both more than you can imagine.

Love,

Mommy

June 2, 2009

Dear Meredith,

Congratulations on your book. I know it will inspire and give hope to many who may be struggling to find peace and will need to be reassured that God is always there.

I applaud you for your strength, bravery and unshakeable faith during some very trying times. Your dad and I know all too well of your many challenges.

I have always loved you and taken such pride in all of your accomplishments. Your strength and inner beauty have amazed me since the day you were born.

Reading this book reminded me of all that we have been through and how God has always been there for us and never let us down.

I pray that God will put this book in the hands of people who need it most and that your story will help them find their way back to the Lord.

Growing up you filled my heart with so much love and pride and I have so much respect and admiration for you as an adult.

You are a wonderful daughter, sister, wife, mother and now author. I know God will continue to bless you and that you will be a blessing to many.

My love always,

Mom

Invite Meredith to speak to your local church, organization, or support group.

For more information, contact
Meredith McNerney

meredithmcnerney@yahoo.com

Be sure to visit Meredith's blog at:

www.facingcancerbook.com

To learn more about
A Message of Hope Cancer Fund, visit:

www.messageofhopecf.org

CPSIA information can be obtained at www.ICGtesting.com
Printed in the USA
LVOW04s2052050914

402695LV00011B/178/P

9 780741 455475